BLIND FAITH

Recognizing and Recovering from Dysfunctional Religious Groups

Kay Marie Porterfield, M.A.

CompCare® Publishers

3850 Annapolis Lane, Suite 100
Minneapolis, Minnesota 55447

©1993 Kay Marie Porterfield
All rights reserved
Published in the United States
by CompCare Publishers

Reproduction in whole or part, in any form, including storage in memory device systems, is forbidden without written permission, except that portions may be used in
broadcast or printed commentary or review when attributed fully to author, illustrator,
and publication by names.

Library of Congress Cataloging–in–Publication Data

Porterfield, Kay Marie
      Blind faith: recognizing and recovering from dysfunctional religious groups/Kay
Marie Porterfield.
         p. cm.
Includes bibliographical references.
ISBN 0–89638–291–5
1. Cults—United States—Controversial literature. 2. Sects—United States—
Controversial literature. 3. Psychology, Religious. 4. United States—Religion—1960. 5.
Ex–cultists—United States.
I. Title.
BP603.P67 1993
291.4' 2—dc20   92–39636
                                                                                                         CIP

Cover design by John Hamilton

Inquiries, orders, and catalog requests should be addressed to:
CompCare Publishers
3850 Annapolis Lane, Suite 100
Minneapolis, MN 55447
Call toll free 800/328–3330
or 612/559–4800

6	5	4	3	2	1
98	97	96	95	94	93

For Dylan, Keith, Tama, and Bonnie, who provided
encouragement, and for Dave G., whose metaphors are always
a source of inspiration

Do not say, "I shall wait until some teacher or Sage comes along, and then I will study with him," or "I will learn from these colleagues who have studied with the master . . . and any questions I have I will ask them and they will answer." Such an opportunity may not present itself to you, and every day time keeps escaping from you.

Rabbi Menahen ben Solomon Ha-Meiri
1249–1306

Other Books by Kay Marie Porterfield

What's a Nice Girl Like You Doing in a Relationship Like This? The Crossing Press, 1991

Violent Voices: 12 Steps to Freedom from Emotional and Verbal Abuse, Health Communications, Inc., 1989

Keeping Promises: The Challenge of a Sober Parent, Hazelden, 1986

Coping with Codependency, Rosen Publishing Group, 1991

Coping with an Alcoholic Parent, Rosen Publishing Group, 1985

Teenage Perspectives: Focus on Addictions and Compulsions, ABC Clio, 1992

CONTENTS

Foreword

Implications of Cults in Light of the Waco, Texas, Tragedy

by Linda Christensen, Ph.D., C.C.D.P.

The tragic events in Waco, Texas, in the spring of 1993, resulting in the fiery deaths of nearly ninety members of the Branch Davidian Cult, show the world the very worst of what can happen when vulnerable people join with a powerful and dangerous religious cult leader. The reasons such a tragedy can occur at all, however, lie within the psyches of people in all times and in all cultures. For in our collective unconscious lies the image of the hero, the messiah.

Humanity's search for heroes and for acts of heroism has led people to far-distant places. In the end, however, our search for a true hero must lead us back to ourselves. Each of us must create meaning for our own lives that empowers, delights, and validates us.

In our desire to live with purpose and meaning, we seek heroes to guide our spiritual search and to act as role models for our behavior. People struggling to live sanely while dealing with extraordinary stress, as well as people seeking deeper meaning while coping with the drudgery of daily routine, find comfort in knowing that others have survived, and even triumphed over, great odds.

When life circumstances arise to test us, we may look to our predecessors for strength and strategies. Martin Luther King, Jr. may serve as a powerful role model for anyone battling racism in the workplace or community. Helen Keller's courage and tenacity may inspire a person whose sight is failing because of glaucoma or diabetes. The legacies of John F. Kennedy, Sally Ride, Sojourner Truth, and other heroes live on to remind us that the human spirit is larger than human pain.

History attests to the passion with which we have taken our journeys to find meaning. Looking "outside" or "up there" to pursue the God of our understanding, we wage holy wars or become martyrs to religious causes. The search for heroes and the desire for union with the Divine, then, are nothing new. What may be new is the desperateness of the search.

People today possess few illusions. In the last quarter-century, our heroes have been assassinated, they have died from overdoses of alcohol and other drugs, and they have fallen from grace into public disgrace on national television. The examples are abundant: the Nixon administration's greed and dishonesty; the deaths of Janis Joplin, Jim Morrison, and Jimi Hendrix, induced by alcohol and other drugs; the abuse of their children by Bing Crosby and Joan Crawford. And, unlike moviegoers of the 1950s and 1960s, we know now to be cynical and a little embarrassed by Rock Hudson's cinematic pining for Doris Day.

When the truth is finally revealed that the chosen few are really just as flawed and as vulnerable as everyone else, the public feels betrayed, sometimes enraged. Eventually, hardened and a bit more cynical, they return with a sigh to their own lives until the next edition of the newspaper or televised newscast gives them someone else in whom to place their hopes.

As Kay Marie Porterfield reports in the pages of this book, people from dysfunctional family systems are particularly in need of heroes, and hence, they are vulnerable to the influence of self-styled saviors such as the Reverend Jim Jones, the Reverend Sun Myung Moon, and David Koresh. The relationship between dysfunctional families and vulnerability to cults is easy to grasp.

As child-development theories illustrate, our first heroes are typically our parents. Newborns grow close to Mother and soon to Father in a symbiotic union that is mutually satisfying. The child is fed, cuddled, and cared for by adults who are big, strong, and trustworthy. The youngster grows through the stages of childhood, while parents and other adult caregivers model appropriate behaviors and provide the love and limits that enable the child to feel safe and special.

These are the theories. Unfortunately, little of these theories apply to families marred by violence, incest, or dependencies on alcohol or other drugs. Instead of having reliable adult role models, children in dysfunctional families grow up with adults who are unable to set consistent limits or to discipline them appropriately. In addition, the adults are absent, sometimes physically, but almost always emotionally.

Often, children do not become close to their parents and never learn to trust them. They do not receive the emotional support or structure they need to become healthy, whole adults. When such important developmental pieces are missing, children become adults who have an emptiness inside, an internal void where love, self-esteem, self-confidence, and wisdom should be. Many search outside themselves throughout their adult lives for things to fill that void. The search may include alcohol and other drugs, unhealthy relationships, sexual promiscuity, food, gambling, or religion.

Emptiness, longing, lack of support, and poorly developed life skills combine with the universally human needs for identification with a hero and union with the Divine to make people who have grown up in dysfunctional systems particularly at risk for whatever sage, guru, or master might come along. The tragedy in Waco, Texas, involving the Branch Davidian Cult led by David Koresh, typifies, in the extreme, what can happen to vulnerable people searching for meaning and wholeness.

Who was David Koresh? We know that he was a high-school-dropout-turned-rock-musician. We know he was raised by a single mother. We know that by age 18 he was involved in a shootout between two branches of the Davidian Cult. What we do not know is how Koresh came to believe himself to be the incarnation of God destined to lead his followers through bloody battle directly to Heaven's gates.

Making guesses about his followers is easier than trying to piece together Koresh's psychological profile. Most of the 120 cult members were white, in their thirties and forties, and from Texas, although some were from Jamaica, England, and Australia. The way they differed from other 30-to-40–year-olds is that they arrived at the Texas compound believing they would be saved from a "satanic" existence on earth and find eternal salvation through Koresh. For some of them, that belief may have stemmed from painful childhood experiences. For others, the desire to identify with a hero may have led them out of mundane lives and into the grip of a convincing, yet deranged, "messiah" in Waco.

Once inside the cult, few people would have been able to withstand Koresh's tactics. Daily life in the cult included repetitious chanting for hours on end, impassioned preaching by the leader, and lengthy periods of sleep and food deprivation. As medical science can attest, powerful brainwashing, combined with just a few days of sleep deprivation and fasting, will push most people close to the edge of sanity, making them highly suggestible. To people in such a state, surrendering wordly goods for the promise of Heaven seems logical.

Living inside the tightly guarded, walled compound also contributed to the power of Koresh and the vulnerability of his followers. Porterfield illustrates in the following pages how isolation is used to persuade and control converts. In the Koresh compound, the members were separated from the familiarity of home and the regularity of daily life. They left behind family and friends who provided not only support, but also ballast and a way to gauge reality. They had no contact with the outside world, and the outside world was allowed no contact with them. Federal agents with bullhorns tried to communicate some semblance of reality and sanity to cult members, but their efforts proved fruitless. The members had been isolated from the mainstream for too long. Followers had become unreachable in a reality created in the demented mind of David Koresh.

Many factors that might be considered innocuous, or at least, typically human, combined to lead to the fifty-one-day standoff and eventually to a nightmare inferno that left eighty-six dead. There were, of course, survivors: twenty-one children and several others released early in the ordeal; five male cult members who were later jailed; and four members who were later hospitalized. We can only guess that these people's hopes for normal lives may have died along with the actual deaths of cult members.

Who is safe from this kind of tragedy? We may all believe we are. Yet Porterfield says we are all at risk. Her experience and research show that while people from dysfunctional familes may be most vulnerable, any of us can fall prey. As you read *Blind Faith*, you will better understand the vulnerability of us all.

In any case, that question is too difficult and complex to answer here. What is more certain is that whenever we give away our power to others we believe to be more intelligent, more skilled, or more holy than we, we place ourselves at risk. When we transform rock musicians, baseball players, or politicians into heroes, we make ourselves vulnerable. When we entrust others with the power of providing our access to the Divine, we give away our own spiritual strength.

We all need to believe we are lovable, strong, and gifted. We need to keep our own power and find joy in our families, friends, and lovers. And we have to continue to deepen our relationship with the God of our understanding in ways that are meaningful, both personally and individually.

Having done that, we will know peace and fulfillment. We will live a life grounded in reality and strength. And we will safeguard ourselves from involvement with pseudo-sages and misguided messiahs.

Introduction

This is a book about childhood spiritual wounding, adult religious abuse, and religious addiction. The following pages explore how and why these things happen and, most importantly, how we can recover from them when they do.

Conceived as an extension of my own healing process, this project is neither a scientific study nor an academic report. I have tried to be fair, but I make no claim to absolute objectivity. That's God's job. Despite the study and research that went into its writing, *Blind Faith* can't help but be colored by my own experiences and perceptions. To clarify any biases I may have, I have included my own story of a year I spent as a member of a dysfunctional religious group.

Those brave people who stepped forward and shared their personal and sometimes painful stories with me are not completely objective either, but I sensed that they, too, have a commitment to fairness. A few were friends, or friends of friends. Some people surfaced through the help of the Cult Awareness Network and Fundamentalists Anonymous. From former nun to ex-Moonie and recovering fundamentalist missionary, the ten people who recount their stories here were courageous in the honesty of their self-searching and in their openness about insights on their transformation from victim to survivor.

Some survivors had discussed their religious abuse before; others spoke freely for the first time. Occasionally the interview process was difficult, for them and for me. I have changed names and some minor background details of these people's lives to respect their privacy and, in some cases, to protect them from reprisals from the organizations they describe.

Those who shared their experiences with me have struggled past most of the betrayal, bitterness, and remorse they once felt; in that sense, they are very special people. Because the majority chose of their own accord to walk away from theri spiritual bondage, they are among the fortunate. The very fact that they spoke freely sets them apart from many victims of religious abuse, as well. All of them value spirituality as an essential component of their lives, despite the heartache they have endured.

The experiences described here do not represent the entire spectrum of religious abuse and addiction. Instead they provide a rare inside look at various ways religious groups can go wrong. These glimpses of others' pain can help seekers identify obstacles in their spiritual paths and take new directions to continue as wiser travelers. No spiritual journey is completely without hazards, but perhaps, as a result of this book, some readers will find their seeking a bit less perilous.

CHAPTER 1

Dreams, Lies, and Promises

I didn't call the number on the homemade flyer posted in the religious section of the bookstore right away, even though it aroused my curiosity. Instead, I scrawled it on the back of an envelope and stuffed it into my purse. I was intrigued by the mysticism classes advertised on the simple notice, but I was cautious, too. After all, Colorado is known for harboring more than its share of off-the-wall religious groups. Hooking up with one of them was the last thing I needed. I had enough headaches coping with a recent divorce, struggling through the galleys of my latest book, and maintaining my recovery.

Like millions of other Americans, I felt a prickle of irritation when glassy-eyed Unification Church members approached me at airports, and I tried my best to ignore the Hare Krishnas as they danced and chanted on busy street corners. In horror I had watched TV reports of the mass suicide in Jonestown, and years later had viewed the news of Jim and Tammy Baker's crumbling empire, wondering how followers could be so easily duped. Like many other people, I was certain that fanatical religious organizations were not part of my world. People who signed on with cults were weird, strange, crazy. No one in her right mind would ever join one, certainly no one as middle class and sensible as me.

All summer I carried the phone number, even though I didn't dial it. For as long as I could remember, the mystical religious experience had pulled me. Reading Teresa of Avila, Meister Eckhart, and John of the Cross had moved me to explore further, and gradually my desire for spiritual growth had taken on a keen intensity, a yearning that wasn't fulfilled in the church I attended. Perhaps the classes might be the answer. Finally curiosity conquered my initial suspicion, and in late August I called. "Come to one class and you will feel like you have found a home," the man who answered said in a heavily accented voice. During our brief conversation he assured me that attending the three-hour sessions once a week would provide me with the focus I needed. Besides meditation, the experience would offer structure and discipline in a centuries-old tradition. "Try it," he advised. "If this way isn't right for you, then there is no reason for you to come back." His suggestion sounded sensible enough, so I agreed to attend the next class.

We met in his sparsely furnished apartment. The format included group meditation, discussion, and a lecture. As this diminutive man spoke about God, his eye contact was so intense, he seemed to be looking into my soul. His attire—too-large corduroy slacks and a white shirt—belied the compelling magnetism he radiated as he smiled patiently, listening to his two other students report their progress. They shared openly, and when my turn came, I was amazed at how easily I expressed my spiritual concerns before these strangers. The depth of intimacy here was far greater than even that of an Alcoholics Anonymous meeting. When the class ended, I felt curiously off balance but reluctant to leave.

That night I recalled a brief discussion I had had with a stranger a year before, about a volume of spiritual stories he carried, a book I had just finished reading. Soon afterward, I had a dream that seemed related to that random encounter. Now I scanned my old journal and read the entry describing the empty room I had entered in my dream, a room I had sensed was a holy place. The white walls, the Oriental rug with a bowl of fruit centered on it, the large windows covered by billowing curtains—all of these details had been present in the teacher's apartment I'd visited hours earlier.

I had dreamed that I stood alone in the center of the room, wondering where everyone had gone. The air around me suddenly glowed and pulsated with a bright light that filled me with a profound peace. After awakening the next morning, I had written, "Even though I don't understand what's going on, something inside me has changed forever." As I reread those words and thought about the mysticism class I had just attended, I remembered a saying I had never fully understood:

"When the student is ready, the teacher will appear." Now the aphorism made perfect sense.

Throughout the fall I continued to attend the weekly classes, open to learning, but still clinging to my old-fashioned, Midwestern suspicion of anything exotic. As the weeks passed, my suspicions diminished. Calmed by the meditation and lulled by the lectures, I did feel as if I'd found the spiritual home I'd been promised when I first called. Although my Methodist missionary ancestors would have looked askance at the chanting and the fasting, those practices had been honored for centuries in the Catholic church. In any case, I was feeling more centered than I had in years. Under such circumstances my mistrust seemed cynically stubborn.

With each week, the class slowly grew in size, and I found myself growing more comfortable. This tradition was a far cry from my rule-bound, ultrastrict childhood church, which had forbidden dancing, movies, and even eating food in a restaurant that served alcohol. Here there were no shaming tirades about original sin and depravity, but simply listening to God speak through our hearts and doing His will. There were no blistering portraits of eternal damnation, only intoxication with the Creator.

Rather than providing me with new information, the weekly lessons confirmed the validity of my own spiritual conclusions from prayer and meditation. My occasional feelings of ecstatic unity with God weren't aberrations; they were glimpses of how human beings are meant to feel. I was excited to know that these transcendent moments didn't have to be random. I could cultivate an awareness of the Divine in my life.

If anyone had told me then that I was involved with a damaging cult or that my mind was being manipulated, I would have shown my degree in counseling and my MENSA membership card and laughed. Whenever I resisted giving up control over my spiritual growth, my teacher seemed to sense my reaction before I could speak and met it with the humble assurance that he didn't consider himself a teacher but a student. True, sometimes the instant emotional intimacy was overwhelming, but I had seen the healing power of such bonds in therapy groups and self-help meetings for years.

Outside weekly classes, there was no active movement, no communal living situation, no fund-raising, no membership recruitment, not even a group name—nothing to trigger caution. In fact, we were instructed to attend weekly worship services in the church of our choice. The core teaching—simplicity, charity, and love—certainly weren't bizarre. Since I knew cults were huge and fanatical collections of folks who dressed oddly and bore strange names, I knew I was perfectly safe.

My teenage son thought otherwise, but he was a notorious critic of anything remotely religious. No one else confronted me because very few people were aware of my involvement. Outsiders couldn't comprehend the mystical intensity of God without personally experiencing it, my teacher advised. The profound interior experiences during meditation and classes were impossible to put into words. To discuss them openly felt like profanity. Since I was coming to enjoy being one of the chosen, it seemed natural to spend less time with my old friends. When the teacher told me and my fellow students to cut ties with all nonspiritual people, I had few ties to cut. Not only did I not mind the isolation, I hardly noticed it.

Although the group gave lip service to free exchange of information, week after week I watched the leader counter new students' queries with an enigmatic smile and the words, "It's mystical. If you have enough faith, you will know." Questioning became a sign of a spiritually undeveloped Western mind and a mark of faithlessness. I didn't have to be told directly to keep my questions to myself. Compliance was how I had survived growing up. It was how I had managed to earn As despite a strong distaste for formal education, and later to endure a verbally abusive marriage. Keeping a low profile was one of the things I did best.

During that time, former friends who saw me on the street commented on how happy I looked. My six months of intensive spiritual work had left me feeling wonderful. Writing flowed as it never had before, and I even picked up the unfinished poems I had set aside after graduating from college more than twenty years before. My book *Violent Voices* had just been accepted by a publisher, and another recovery book simmered in the back of my mind, a book I would need to start soon.

Despite my joy, I was unprepared when my teacher told me privately that I was far more advanced than any of his other students. He had taught us that spiritual development wasn't linear, that one student couldn't be ahead of another; but I put the bewilderment aside and, like a teacher's pet or a favored child, I was flattered beyond belief. It took months to understand that it was belief in my own self-worth that I was being flattered beyond.

One icy January day, I received another summons. This time, as I sat on the thick Persian rug drinking tea from a gold-rimmed glass, the teacher fixed me in his penetrating gaze and said, "I think you should know I absolutely do not believe in psychology of any kind." His voice resonated with a hard-edged reproof that left me reeling with confusion and shame.

"Sometimes therapy is a Band-Aid," I agreed, "but if it holds us together so we can get to the emergency room where we can take care of our spiritual needs, is it wrong? Without AA and therapy, I would probably be dead or living in a mental hospital today. I had to work through a lot of emotional stuff before I was ready to come to you."

"No matter. I am completely against psychology. That is what I wanted to tell you," he concluded and dismissed me. He permitted no further discussion, but the implication of his scolding was inescapable. In exchange for my spiritual growth, he required me to turn my back on the study and writing that I considered a gift from God.

I had always had a heartfelt knowledge that I was, and I am, meant to write. How could I have been so wrong? How could I be the top student one minute and damned the next? I tried to rationalize the teacher's harsh position by viewing it as a semantic misunderstanding. Maybe he meant Freudian psychology. His English wasn't the best, I rationalized, and I knew that other religious leaders had written books about the link between spirituality and psychology, mind and soul. In fact, one in this particular tradition was a psychiatrist. When I called a long-term student to help sift through my confusion, he told me, "You probably heard him wrong. You're making a big deal out of nothing." I knew I hadn't, and I wasn't.

Perhaps my teacher was testing me, purposely provoking me to determine the purity of my intent and the depth of my surrender; or maybe I was being pushed off balance with mixed messages in order to gain a new perspective and sever ties with ego attachments and unhealthy defenses. I resolved to be patient and to try to stretch my consciousness to fit the dilemma.

During the next few weeks my patience was tested to the limit as the class heard lecture after lecture against psychology, a term that was never defined. The teacher punctuated these warnings with jibes aimed directly at me, including the repeated misidentification of me as a psychologist. My ears burned with humiliation, and my gut burned with anger.

The follow-your-own-heart rule was still voiced, but from the intensity of the scapegoating, I knew I was allowed to follow my heart only in the direction my teacher chose for me. To resist or even question one part of his teaching, he made clear, was to reject the whole. After several sleepless nights, I decided it would be far better for me to fall from this rigid man's graces than from my Maker's. Rather than change my career, I would quit the group.

No sooner had I made my decision than the teacher telephoned. "I need your advice," he said, his voice hushed. "Before I came to this country, I was told by my teacher to start a center for service. It has come to me that we will help the poor. Now I am ready to do that." He paused. "I have told no one else. Because you are a writer, I want you to help me find a name for our center to serve the poor." Assuming that his culture prevented a man from admitting to a woman that he had erred, I took his request as an apology and in a rush of relief and renewed fervor, I pulled out my thesaurus.

Even though I tried to deny my uneasiness, I couldn't help but feel extremely uncomfortable. At the next class, the teacher announced, "There are dark, invisible forces in the world. They will try to stop our progress. We must constantly guard against them through prayer and meditation." I didn't wonder why he stared at me so intently when he spoke. By now I was convinced that he could read my mind, and I was both ashamed of my doubts and afraid of this man who was my spiritual mentor. I wished I hadn't been singled out to share his secret.

I tried to escape my emotional turmoil and stay in his good graces by designing brochures to attract new students to the classes, but my doubts only grew. Internally I cringed at his sudden insistence on hard sell and his claim that his teaching techniques were unique in the Western Hemisphere. It bothered me that donations were no longer sufficient. Now he planned to charge 20 dollars a class and to recruit high-income students rather than the poor intellectuals and college students he was currently attracting. Finally I spoke up and expressed concern about basing important decisions on the need for more money.

"In my country people offer a spiritual teacher jewels and oriental rugs," he responded. "When one is sincere in his longing for God, he finds the money somewhere. The path to God is difficult," he continued. "People in your country want everything to come easily. They do not put a high value on holy things."

In many ways, what he said was true. Certainly my own path to sobriety had been punctuated with bouts of yearning for shortcuts and an easy way out. Maybe I was setting myself up for a spiritual relapse now.

I began to feel even worse when I learned that, although the teacher had told students that he would save their donations for future spiritual work, it appeared instead that he had spent the money for his own living expenses. How he managed funds didn't bother me, but the lying did. I no longer felt that I could trust him even though he insisted we all must.

Without revealing the details of my suspicions, I discussed my discomfort with the student whom I respected most. "Our teacher is always giving us the lessons we need to learn," he told me. "He knows what is best for us. You need to accept that." Maybe developing an immunity to hypocrisy and betrayal was my lesson. I tried harder.

An executive plan book appeared on the teacher's kitchen table, and he began tossing around terms like *worldwide ministry* and *market share* when he referred to his new project. Yet he continued to tell us every week, "I have no interest in worldly things. I have no desire to be famous."

Soon after the project to help the poor was announced to the group, it was amended to include the establishment of a church. Next, the teachings changed. Now as new students entered the class, they were not instructed to attend worship services outside the group. When I mentioned my own involvement with the American Society of Friends, I faced stony silence from the very person who had urged me to become more involved with my faith in the first place.

The teacher did not pressure me to donate money. Instead, he demanded that I ask my business contacts for the names of millionaires who might fund his center. It was important, he said, to find people who would donate money with no strings attached, people who would not be directly involved. When I stalled, the teacher told me with a raised eyebrow that, although I should follow the dictates of my heart, loving God meant doing everything to serve Him and carry out His will. During class he blatantly courted new students who appeared wealthy, boasting that the group even had a "famous" writer, me, in its midst.

None of his other students seemed troubled by the contradictions between his teachings and actions. Whenever I tentatively expressed doubt, they advised me that crazy wisdom was a teaching tool, and that truly enlightened men never played by society's rules. Because God always acted through them, they could do no wrong. Ethics were designed solely for the unenlightened. After our conversations I wondered what was wrong with me and believed I must be spiritually retarded, inept, and blind to the truth this holy man was trying to share.

Precisely when I once more gathered enough courage to break with the group, I received another call to sit on the rug and drink tea with the master. "Someday you will help translate and edit the book I have written," he told me. "But first we need to work on the church. I want you to know, though, that in the future we will earn salaries from the ministry. You will be the head of our publishing company. For now the service you can do for God is writing letters to wealthy people for me." Although his timing was once more perfect, the carrot he dangled before me was all wrong. I remained silent.

"A teacher and a student have a very special spiritual bond which can never be broken," he continued, his voice low and vibrant, his eyes narrowed. "The teacher's soul becomes one with that of the student, so that their thoughts and feelings are one." I felt filled with his unwavering gaze. He didn't say another word, nor did he seduce me in a sexual sense; that was completely unnecessary. It was my spirit that was being sought and appropriated. Freedom seemed impossible, as though my soul would never be my own again.

Zombielike, I embraced work as a drug of choice. Soon my time, energy, and attention centered on the group and the new church so completely that I seldom thought or talked of anything else. My writing suffered because of this obsession and, although I continued to be physically present for my teenage son, often I was mentally absent.

The teacher's second-in-command, my friend, began calling me every day, sometimes two or three times a day. Although I was sure this kind and gentle man's concern with my well-being and my loyalty stemmed from genuine caring, I resented his worry that my "analytical mind" was leading me astray. Each day he counseled that I needed more faith, more trust. Once I had it, I would know the truth, and my concerns would resolve themselves.

Between the teacher's monitoring, spiritual homework from the classes, meditation, and working to help start the church, I was as hooked as I had ever been on alcohol eleven years before and equally miserable. Like the waning solace in my final encounters with alcohol, the euphoria I had felt earlier was now increasingly elusive. Even so, I didn't think I could survive without the teacher or his classes. I tried to see my inner agony as a sign indicating that I was dying to myself, a condition outlined in a variety of religious teachings, including the Christianity I'd been raised on.

I remember one day complaining to a woman who was peripherally connected to our group. I said I felt like an animal caught in a trap, frantically gnawing through its own leg to escape. She replied that perhaps it was a trap of love. The word *coercion* popped into my mind, but according to the unspoken belief system I'd slowly incorporated as my own, escape from this snare would mean spiritual death.

Two weeks later, the leader who claimed my soul left on an extended trip to his homeland. Beginning the night after he boarded the airplane, my sleep was wracked with nightmares. In one of them the master ferociously urged an army of white horses and a team of roan horses to fight to the death. When it was over, the field was covered with blood, dust, and carcasses. The only living thing left was my teacher, who grinned through the haze and the stench with pride at the carnage he had created for the sake of satisfying his blood lust.

In another dream, he was lecturing. As the listening crowd grew in number, he diminished in size until his assistant and I had to hold a huge magnifying glass in front of him wherever he walked so that no one would realize he was only six inches tall. In the dream I left to become a Mormon.

During my waking moments I was convinced my nightmares were caused by the mysterious, dark forces I had been warned about. I persisted, even though the day before the teacher's return, one of my female classmates, a woman I had been instructed to consider my spiritual sister, woke me up at 6:00 A.M. with a threatening and obscene phone call. That, too, was probably a dark force at work.

By now I was so disconnected from my feelings and values that when I was ordered to use my research skills to infiltrate the fastest-growing churches in the area to learn their secrets, I said I would try. I was determined to live with yet another paradox when my teacher told me that the Twelve Steps were as ridiculous and useless as psychology, that the possibility of experiencing a spiritual awakening from following them was out of the question. I began to question whether my recovery had, in fact, led to a spiritual awakening or whether I had deluded myself.

Ironically, a relatively minor incident prompted me to finally walk away from the group. I had written a series of articles to gain some publicity for the new church and had submitted them to both my teacher and his overprotective assistant for their final approval. Each gave me an okay, so I sent the pieces out. Only when it was too late to make changes did the second-in-command tell me he had problems with the work I had done. When I asked for clarification, he refused to give it. I felt as though I were 6 years old and back in my family of origin. Nothing I did was right. It was wrong to have or express feelings, wrong to disobey authority or even question it, wrong to be an individual, wrong to set boundaries, wrong to want privacy or clear communication. I was tired of the secrets and sick of being manipulated.

Once my denial crumbled and I recognized the oppression of the shame-bound system for what it was, I couldn't believe any longer that God wanted me to be imprisoned in this dysfunctional religious family. I told the assistant I needed to take time off from working on the center to focus on my recovery process.

When the master called me, his voice shook with fury. "What have you done?" he shouted. "This project is very important to me; you know that! It is a promise I made to God and I will allow nothing to stop it, nothing! Haven't you learned anything I tried to teach you?" At that moment I regressed emotionally to a 4-year-old torn between my desire to please an omnipotent father figure and an inherent need to assert my independence from him.

In keeping with the melodrama that had characterized my life the preceding year, the final time I sat cross-legged on the rich red rug, an eclipse began to darken the August moon. This time there were no smiles or tea, and certainly no sympathy. All business, my teacher asked me for my complaints. With tears in my eyes, I listed them and tried to explain that, although I remained devoted to God, because I grew up with a chronically depressed mother and a workaholic father from which I was still recovering, I could not sanely tolerate half-truths and mixed messages; nor could I deny that therapy and Twelve Step programs had helped me. To do that would deny the validity of my experience and jeopardize my sobriety.

One by one he addressed my concerns. First, he declared I had not sincerely chosen to study. If I had, childhood trauma would have absolutely no influence on me as an adult. Moreover, my points were meaningless because, as of that evening, I was no longer a member of the group. "Since I am a spiritual teacher," he continued, "I knew everything you would say before you spoke. I have known you would leave all along." Finally, he concluded, his voice icy, "As you will remember, I do not believe in psychology."

Like any addict cut off from her substance, I plunged into a miserably intense period of withdrawal. For weeks after my departure, I felt aimless, spiritually uprooted, unsure whether I had abandoned God or He had abandoned me. I questioned whether my decision to assert myself might have a profound, even eternal, impact. Left without a solid support network, I was now alone, abandoned, and depressed.

My concentration faltered, and I had many incidents of what exit counselors call "floating." I would hear my teacher's voice telling me I had made an irreparable mistake or catch occasional whiffs of the rose incense he used to burn before class. Because of the psychic energy between us, I was afraid he might still be trying to control me. The post-divorce issues I'd swept aside a year ago returned with a vengeance. To compound my fear, hurt, and anger, I felt stupid for having joined in the first place and spent hours shaming myself for being so gullible. A victim of spiritual rape, I felt more betrayed than I had known was possible, and I was convinced that I had invited and deserved the abuse.

That fall I started to work through these issues, and shortly after I ran into my former teacher in the same bookstore where I had seen his poster the year before. He sat on a bench smiling his mystical smile, his lap stacked with books about shame, codependency, and sexual addiction. For an instant, I believed he had softened his antirecovery position, but as we talked, I learned that his mind and his heart remained closed.

A month later he called me and forbade me ever to set foot in his church again. If I saw him in a public place, I was to pretend not to recognize him. I listened, stunned, as he told me I could read books or continue to attend that other church I had joined if I wanted to grow. Since I had never fully submitted to him as a teacher, this banishment should have meant nothing to me. His tone seemed compassionate, but the content of his words sounded as though he had read textbook instructions for shredding the self-esteem of a recovering adult child.

Recalling the image of him poring over recovery books, I understood that despite his skepticism of psychology, he had found exactly what he needed during his book-browsing, information-twisting excursions. The same information he was using to hurt me could lure others into the group. The larger-than-life idol I had created over the past months shrank to the six-inch human of my dream.

As I hung up the phone, a surge of anger shot through me, healthy anger at his arrogance and deception, at his ego and ambition, all masquerading under the guise of a spiritual leader. I felt sorrow for his future students who would be seduced by this calculated facade and the contrived energy he projected. He would exploit their hunger as he had mine. They, too, would be used and then discarded if they interfered with the grandiose scheme. He would leave them in the end with only shattered dreams, lies, and broken promises.

In the months that followed, I read everything I could find about spiritual manipulation, trying to put my experience into a meaningful context. I learned that I was lucky: My affiliation had been short term, and I hadn't lived in a communal situation or been drained of financial resources. However, I had not needed to join a large, name-brand cult, change my name, shave my head, or stay up nights selling flowers to be duped in a spiritual confidence game.

Dysfunctional religious groups come in all shapes and sizes, from full-blown megacults to the tiny, anonymous groups that are currently experiencing a dramatic upsurge in America. Their teachings range from the exotic and esoteric to down-home Bible thumping. I discovered that I had been part of what experts call a precult, a group in the process of forming. Like any relationship, religious organizations are not static. When I began attending the classes, they were firmly rooted in spiritual principles. As the focus toward a worldwide ministry progressed, the dysfunctional dynamics overwhelmed the teachings. Survival as a member was impossible without crippling codependency and discarding previously held values and beliefs. Since psychotherapy was prohibited, a common cult practice, the damaging patterns were not only allowed to continue, but elevated to signs of spiritual advancement. Of course, I felt at home in the classes. In a profound sense, I had returned to my psychically ill family of origin.

The more I studied cult methods, the more striking were the parallels between destructive religious groups and dysfunctional families. The characteristics were all there: the authority figure who posed as an alternately stern and loving parent; the hateful sibling rivalry; the unpre-dictability; and the rule by shame. Certain feelings were declared taboo. It was forbidden to discuss conflicts and openly work toward resolution. The system was closed, with little opportunity to confirm reality and no checks and balances.

During my year of spiritual insanity, visitor after visitor dropped in for one or two classes and left, never to be heard from again. All who stayed came from dysfunctional families or were sober alcoholics. Although we had not set out to be abused, once enmeshed we didn't notice shaming and manipulation because we were used to them. We craved the healing of our childhood wounds; instead those wounds were reopened and deepened. I wondered how many other recovering people and adult children had shared my experiences.

I took the risk of being judged odd, like one of the Krishnas or Moonies I had so easily dismissed before, and I began to share my story. I discovered that several people I knew had been involved at one time or another in a dysfunctional religious group. These were bright, successful, interesting, and idealistic people who had "lost" several months or years of their lives. They all carried a residue of shame and kept their past victimization by religious abusers hidden. Many were reluctant to talk about the past. It seemed to me more than coincidence that several of the people I spoke with had suffered from childhood trauma, were raised in dysfunctional families, or had grappled with addiction.

Not all victims of spiritual abuse are the products of dysfunctional families, of course. Religious manipulators selectively use a variety of psychological techniques to hold sway over their followers. No one is completely immune to them. Once trapped inside a dysfunctional spiritual group, one can suffer such severe damage that the aftermath closely resembles the emotional fallout from incest or rape.

The spiritual coercion and betrayal I experienced penetrated my core more deeply and did more damage to me than anything in my life before or since. Not only had my boundaries, my values, and my trust been routinely assaulted, I felt as though my ability to relate to God had been ripped from me. For months I stopped praying and meditating. The thought of setting foot in a church made me want to cry, as if God Himself had violated me.

As I struggled to heal, I slowly worked through my categorical, black-and-white thinking and came to understand that human failing, rather than Divine malevolence, had twisted the group's dynamics, money, and power into objects of worship. To discard the valid mystical teachings I had learned during the first months of my sojourn or to embrace their opposite didn't make sense.

Time granted me the perspective to see that. Although this teacher might have started out a sincere and godly man, his unresolved emotional issues and messianic delusions drove him to create a group setting where he could get the adoration and obedience he craved. I had been an enabler in that process. Still, to judge all spiritual teachers from this one man would be as rigid a judgment as his unbending condemnation of psychology.

I remembered my dream of the white room where nothing mattered except for me and the source of light: no teacher, no students, no rituals, no routines. I knew that to deny or discount the transcendent spiritual experiences I'd been blessed with throughout my life would be a mistake. The mystical, ecstatic experience of God is simply a part of who I am. It was the misguided meaning imposed upon my sacred internal adventures, not the adventures themselves, that was destructive. Prayer, meditation, and worship were, and continue to be, valid and very effective tools for knowing the Divine. Their calculated misuse was no reason to give them up.

As I read about religious addiction and abuse, I grew increasingly frustrated with much of the material. Some authors labeled any religion other than Christianity as a cult. Others denounced mystical religious experiences as hallucinations. There was a need for a more thoughtful and temperate book about discerning destructive spiritual groups and teachers, a book for people like me. Because so many of us in recovery are consciously working on spirituality, we needed a book that addressed our issues, too, and the role our Higher Power played in healing from addiction and traumatic childhood. Since growing up in dysfunctional families left us feeling as if we had holes in our souls, the book I searched for had to talk about our unique vulnerabilities. And it needed to be a book that focused on group dynamics rather than promoting one belief system as the only way to God.

It finally dawned on me that if such a book were to come into being, I would have to be the one to write it. I am not a psychologist, although I have a graduate degree in counseling, nor am I a theologian. Since I am just a journalist, I felt shaky about my credentials, afraid to take on the responsibility. As I sat at the word processor, blocked and staring at the blank screen, my fears became a refrain: Who am I to write this book? Who am I to write this book?

When the phone rang, I jumped. The caller was the editor of a regional recovery paper, thanking me for unwittingly sending her an article just in time to save her from a publishing nightmare. "The therapist we interviewed for the cover story called right before we were going to press," she said. "She told us to cancel the piece because she's involved in some religious group, and she took back everything she said about recovery two weeks ago; she doesn't believe any of it now. I don't understand what happened!" I understood. This time when I sat down at my computer, the words came easily.

Who am I to write this book? I am a seeker who was badly hurt. As Kahlil Gibran wrote, "I have learned silence from the talkative, tolerance from the intolerant, and kindness from the unkind; yet strangely, I am ungrateful to these teachers." I am a student who, with the help of my Higher Power, is learning to get back up when I stumble and to feel gratitude for all of my teachers in this class called life.

CHAPTER TWO

Dysfunctional Groups Defined

—Two thousand members of the Church Universal and Triumphant, acting on a revelation from leader Elizabeth Claire Prophet, gather at church headquarters in Montana to await World War III. Their preparations include not only moving into bomb shelters, but amassing a large cache of semiautomatic and assault rifles. Eventually Prophet's husband is arrested and sentenced to spend a month in jail for smuggling a truckload of .50-caliber machine guns into the compound.

—A TV reporter in Tucson is sent to interview the leader of the Ahura Mazda Self-Realization Church for a segment on Islamic religions. She becomes his follower and lover, eventually writing thousands of dollars in bad checks, running up $25,000 on credit cards, and losing her job. She receives probation for her crime, but her spiritual mentor is jailed for allegedly firebombing a TV station and bank.

—A Hare Krishna leader of a 4,000-acre commune in West Virginia is faced with a grand jury indictment for murder and racketeering. In addition to trying to kill two former members of the group, he is accused of authorizing kidnappings and beatings of other members.

—In Racine, Wisconsin, testimony in a custody case reveals child abuse practiced in a fifty-member, Bible-based group called The Family. Leader Larry Yarber, a former karate instructor who calls himself a prophet of God, denies the allegations, but once justified this practice in a newspaper interview: "The Bible tells you to beat your child and anyone who doesn't do what the Bible says, doesn't believe in Jesus Christ."

Newspapers across the nation are peppered with dramatic stories about religious groups gone wrong. Even though these tales are unsettling, most people find them as far removed from the reality of daily life as I once did. Believers can get so wrapped up in twisted religious systems that they lie, cheat, steal, and even kill in the name of God. Repugnant as that fact is, such aberrations do happen.

We like to believe that people who join these organizations aren't a bit like us. Maybe they're not very smart, or perhaps they've been completely brainwashed into following a demented leader. Then we relax into smug certainty. Nothing that gruesome or demeaning, nothing that frightening or dramatic could happen in our lives. But our sense of security is a false one. People who find themselves in the clutches of repressive religious groups tend to be intelligent, well educated, idealistic, and middle class. They are just like the people we know. They are just like us.

In 1982, *The New York Times* estimated that 3,000 destructive cults existed in the United States, involving 3 million people. Cult experts are convinced that the phenomenon is growing, albeit less noticeably than during the seventies. New groups are often small and hidden from media attention. Since recruiting efforts usually target people in the midst of life transitions, not only are teenagers and the elderly the objects of proselytizing, so are people facing divorce or midlife crisis. Those of us recovering from chemical dependency, eating disorders, codependency, or traumatic childhoods are easy prey as well, since we ache to make spiritual sense of our pain.

A belief in a Higher Power—be that power God, Allah, the Goddess, Buddha, or Vishnu—provides the meaning we need. Conscious contact with the Divine is inspiring, comforting, and growth promoting, and the desire to find or create community with others who share our beliefs and spiritual goals is a natural urge. In the hands of the twisted, however, the groups in which we worship, learn, and socialize have tremendous potential to support our spiritual growth. In some cases, however, they can wreak havoc on our mental health.

Spiritual Choices

We live in an unprecedented age of spiritual choices. A person may enter a Native American sweat lodge on Friday, take a Zen meditation workshop on Saturday, and attend a traditional Episcopal worship service on Sunday morning, reserving the afternoon for a New Age lecture on raising consciousness with crystals. The boom in charismatic churches, new faiths, Eastern religions, and the rise of the New Age movement provide varied avenues for spiritual growth.

These choices may be exciting, confusing, and more than a little overwhelming, since not all of the possibilities open to us promote growth. No longer can we rely on the old frames of reference our parents used or those we learned in childhood, to discriminate between the organizations that would help us and those with potential to cause harm.

For one thing, the teachings, practices, and even the way religious groups are organized may be unsettling if they are new to us or are rooted in another culture. Since we're not sure what to expect, we try to be tolerant and strive to accept everything we're told on faith. In groups led by a living teacher or enlightened master, we may be uncertain about how to define submission and discipleship. To confuse matters further, we're not really sure how to distinguish an enlightened person from a leader who merely claims illumination.

Finally whether the religion in question is a version of charismatic Christianity, Sufism, Zen, or a new mysticism, one of the primary techniques used under the guise of helping us connect with God is altering consciousness. Fasting, chanting, and meditating, although part of the Western spiritual tradition, historically have been limited to a few committed people or to those who made a full-time commitment to religious life. The average seeker with little knowledge of mystical experiences may find it difficult to differentiate between the wishful thinking of ego from true spiritual vision.

When we first begin to awaken to the potential richness of our relationship to God, we are often confused, as well, about how to integrate into daily life the experiences we have when we meditate, intensely pray, or retreat to the mountains. Our confusion about the meaning of our experiences and what to do next makes novices vulnerable to outside interpretations. The interpreters we choose may foster our deepening spirituality, or they may use our private and profound experiences for their own selfish ends, leaving emotional devastation in their wake.

All those on the spiritual path have the potential to be part of groups that provide new understanding and a deeper relationship with the Higher Power. In the search for those groups, anyone may stumble into a manipulative group intent on controlling not only time and money but mind and heart. Ironically, the chance of involvement in manipulative groups increases dramatically when people arrogantly believe themselves immune to high-pressure spiritual sales tactics. Thinking that they are too wise to be duped, they foolishly ignore common sense, and before they know what has happened, sign away their souls.

Toward a New Definition of Spiritual Abuse

The word *cult* brings to mind simplistic, either/or categories. Whether we define a cult as the fringe group in today's headlines or as any organization adhering to teachings different from our own beliefs, such black-and-white thinking is dangerous and self-deceptive. In the first place, it fans the flames of religious bigotry, allowing us to totally discount the positive experiences people have in religious organizations that don't fit securely into our view of mainstream American culture. In addition, there is a popular tendency to categorize any belief system that is new or different as a cult, despite the fact that most of the world's major religions, Christianity included, technically began as cults.

This us-and-them approach also confines our notion of what constitutes spiritual abuse to a narrow spectrum of perpetrators. When we read about a Sunday school teacher arrested for molesting his students or a priest removed from his church for striking a parishioner because she played the tambourine out of turn, we don't want to believe it. The newspapers can't be telling the truth, we may decide, because we're sure such terrible things only happen in fringe groups.

Stories about religious abuse that make headlines are only the tip of the iceberg of spiritual abuse. The woman quietly seduced by her pastor during a counseling session and the man whose well-meaning parents used to spank him with a Bible when he misbehaved are victims just as the teenager who starves herself to raise funds so her guru can buy a limousine. The lonely, elderly TV viewer, talked out of her life savings by a TV evangelist who convinces her she is buying a reserved seat in heaven, is every bit as victimized as the entrepreneur who sells his business and gives the proceeds to a man he believes is Christ. Religious organizations don't have to officially qualify as cults in order to leave spiritual bruises on adults or children.

For that reason books that merely warn readers away from a list of specific religions are not as useful as they appear to be on the surface. Religious groups are also constantly changing. Some that began on a positive foundation later turn into hotbeds of manipulation and greed. Others initially wield incredible power over their members but then weaken and change their internal structure or disband after the death of a charismatic leader. Rarely do large groups consistently promote or constrict growth in every area of the organization. Even if a certain mainline denomination's reputation is without major blemishes, and it functions well as a whole, a particular congregation may be punitive and abusive.

The more general conception of dysfunctional religious groups describing ecclesiastical organizations that inhibit rather than promote their members' spiritual growth loosens the hold of old mind-sets. When we look at a continuum of behaviors and outcomes rather than judging church groups by rigid stereotypes, we understand that groups change over time; they can be mega-organizations or tiny one- or two-person cells. Committees or classes may be abusive within a larger organization which, for the most part, enhances growth. Dysfunction is not limited to fringe groups whose members wear ostrich feathers in their hair and chant the phone book backward every full moon nor to oh-so-proper prayer and Bible discussion meetings. Under certain circumstances our families may become dysfunctional religious groups, too.

Our Side of the Equation

This way of viewing religion provides valuable clues to whether a particular group helps or harms individuals, no matter how it is labeled. The broader definition enables believers to figure out whether involvement with a particular religious organization is right for them at a given point in their lives, rather than endorsing or condemning it for all time. After all, the very spiritual groups that promote growth for some, restrict others. And the groups that helped a person unfold spiritually yesterday may seem like prisons tomorrow.

Whether or not a religious group works for us depends a good deal on the expectations members bring to the encounter. When asked to share their views about the ideal function of religious groups, people gave many different answers. They wanted religious groups to

- provide spiritual leadership.

- answer their questions.

- offer a strong, consistent foundation on which to build lives, actions, and beliefs.

- provide a format for regular worship.

- formulate ethics.

- serve as a concrete symbol of love.

- be like a family.

- give social opportunities for people with a common moral code.

- serve as a support system.

- nurture the individual.

- expand awareness of God.

- encourage questioning and learning.

- provide excitement.

- be a source of joy, life, love.

- help people through transitions.

- evoke peaceful feelings and foster love.

- teach people to cope with everyday life.
- be supportive and enable people to form their own religious beliefs.
- comfort people.
- serve as a focus for identity.
- glorify God.
- teach beliefs.
- reinforce the beliefs people already have.
- provide an opportunity for discussion in a context of shared belief.
- offer a frame of reference for moral purpose and the meaning of life.
- help define and refine personal values.

As this list suggests, everybody wants something different. It is impossible for a spiritual group to meet all of these needs and keep every potential member happy. What a religious organization can do depends on a person's emotional development. Even though a seeker thinks he or she has joined a religious group to find mystical experiences, if the real need to be accepted into a social group and to have friends hasn't been adequately met, socialization is the hidden motivator. Loosely knit groups that focus mainly on worship rather than fellowship simply won't satisfy.

A person who is terrified of earning a living and being independent may look for groups to meet physical needs and provide the rules and structure, while under the delusion of wanting to learn more about God. In that case, communal living arrangements may be a group's primary appeal. People who do not accept or feel good about themselves affiliate with a religious organization seeking self-esteem, so they are attracted to uplifting sermons and displays of affection.

To choose groups and teachers wisely, seekers need to consider their part in the interaction and the emotional needs they bring to the spiritual search. An honest awareness of one's motivations and goals is critical if judgment is to remain unclouded by denial and delusion.

Religious Addiction

Depending on the needs we attempt to fill with religion, it may not be the group that goes astray, but us. Our compulsive spiritual questing can drive us into religious addiction, forming an unhealthy relationship with a healthy group. We may use prayer and meditation, ritual, and doctrine like drugs. We give our lives over completely, not to God, but to a group of believers or a religious leader who may not even want or ask for such dependency from us.

Spiritual growth is a necessary part of the healing process for people in recovery from addiction or abusive childhoods. The support of a renewed connection with God may also be the only thing that gets us through a bitter divorce, a medical problem, the loss of a job, the death of a family member, or an identity crisis. Ironically, at the very points in our lives when we feel the need for the structure of a religious organization most in order to reaffirm our relationship with God, we are the most vulnerable to injury by unscrupulous groups. At the same time, we're carrying emotional baggage that makes us prone to turning involvement with the healthiest of groups into an addiction.

Group Hubris

Once upon a time, far away, God and the devil were walking down the road when something beautiful and shiny lying on the ground caught God's attention. He bent down to pick it up and held it in His hand to examine it. "Hmmm, what do you have there?" asked the devil, his voice thick with greed. "The truth," answered God. "Here," said the devil, reaching out his hand and snatching it away. "Give it to me and I'll organize it for you!"

Religious organizations, no matter how holy their purpose, are not perfect. They are all comprised of flesh-and-blood people, complete with very human flaws and aspirations. Regardless of the truth inherent in a group's teachings, its dynamics can go awry. Even though clergy, lay leaders, and members sincerely aspire to serve God, any group has the potential to become spiritually abusive—from the Lutheran Ladies' Sewing Circle to the New Age past-life regression group advertised in the newspaper.

The creation of worldly institutions rooted in sacred beliefs is not a simple task. In any religious organization, tension is bound to exist between the sacred or vertical dimension and the social or horizontal dimension of the group. A relationship with God is highly personal. To define it is as difficult as nailing jelly to a tree. The harder we try to pin it down, the more elusive it becomes. Ideally the tension between the sacred and the social provides a dynamic system of checks and balances, promoting synthesis and growth, rather than stopping it. It provides a framework for experiences with the sacred and guides integration into daily life.

The balance between these two poles is never static, either for the groups as a whole or for individual members. John, a former member of the Unification Church who left several years ago, says, "In the beginning the connection I felt in the church was vertical, primarily with God. The longer I was there, the more horizontal it became, with brothers and sisters and leaders. So my spirituality increasingly became something outside myself, something I had to put on a face for, and it lost its momentum and energy."

One purpose of religion is to preserve spiritual experience and communicate tradition to others. The creeds, rituals, and routines are all carefully written down. A hierarchy of priests or ministers and lay members is established. Codes of behavior are developed, and approved methods or technologies for relating to God are solidified. The group develops an identity, believing that its way differs from the way of others.

When the balance tips too far toward maintaining the social structure, though, a group risks failing to meet its primary stated function— to foster the individual's opportunity to connect with the Higher Power. In organizations that emphasize mainly the horizontal dimension, whether in the form of social gatherings, social change, fund-raising, or conversion of new members, attention may be diverted from God.

Rather than being living symbols that reflect the individual sacred experience, or a means of fostering conscious connection with God, sometimes groups and practices become ends in themselves. The old tale of the guru and his cat dramatizes this point. Whenever the master lectured, the tabby wouldn't leave him alone. Its purring and meowing distracted the newer students, who had yet to hone their powers of concentration. To restore order, the guru instructed that, before his lecture, someone was to find the cat, put a collar on it, and tie it to a tree in another part of the ashram. This was done each day.

Shortly afterward, the guru died. Each time his successor lectured, the cat was dutifully tied to the tree where it had always been tied. Eventually the cat died. Students bought a replacement, a tabby with markings exactly like those of its predecessor, and tied this new cat to the tree before lectures. Old students left the ashram; new ones came. Gurus died and new ones took over. Still, a cat was invariably tied to a tree before lectures began. When a new student questioned the strange practice, he was told, "This is a religious ritual set forth by our founder. It is necessary for our teaching. Unless a cat is tied to this particular tree, we will never find enlightenment."

People who belong to a group need to be aware of the constant tension between the connection with God and the culture of rules and routines. If a group is in balance, its members have a responsibility to stay in balance themselves. Our personal relationship with God breathes life into the religious institutions to which we belong. Those same religious institutions can give grounding to our mystical experiences, enabling us to live them out within the context of community.

Do They Practice What They Preach?

The hypocrisy of groups that practice the opposite of what they preach is not confined to cults, new religions, or old ones. Schools and even alcohol treatment centers sometimes subordinate primary goals to either building the organization or maintaining its status quo. Schools may sacrifice students' education to keep incompetent teachers on staff and a burned-out administration in power. A treatment center that focuses more on obtaining state funding and insurance payments than on helping clients overcome addiction compromises healing. In the case of a dysfunctional religious group, the cost is even higher. There it is the members' relationship with God that becomes the sacrifice offered to the group's stability.

Soul-scarring religious organizations don't advertise as such. They loudly talk a good doctrine, while at the same time subtly nurturing dependency and suffocating independent thinking. Only when members investigate the group's inner workings do they begin to uncover the hidden agendas. By that time members may not leave easily.

Regarding a leader as an all-knowing, all-powerful parent figure, and themselves as among the elect, makes it more difficult to defect. Even though members suffer emotional anguish if they stay, cutting ties with a dysfunctional religious group can seem tantamount to committing spiritual suicide.

Before pledging themselves to an organization based on teachings alone, seekers must look beyond doctrine for common characteristics dysfunctional groups share. Evidences of a trait or two is not a fail-safe sign that a particular body of believers is on the wrong track. It does suggest, however, that potential for dysfunction exists. Unless the religious organization is making a conscious effort to address negative potential, chances are that abuse will develop.

Characteristics of Dysfunctional Religious Groups

A powerful charismatic leader who claims divinity or infallibility. A religious teacher or leader doesn't need to claim to be God incarnate in order to be dangerous. Claim of ultimate religious authority also creates an environment for abuse of power. Once members buy into the belief that someone outside themselves knows all there is to know about spirituality, they may be willing to act against their own values to gain that person's favor and attention. Rather than respectfully submitting themselves conditionally to a teacher or guide, they surrender their common sense and ability to think critically.

Authoritarian power structure. Leaders who assume total power to validate or negate the self-worth of devotees keep their followers in line by manipulating the hope of salvation or enlightenment as well as the fear of condemnation or rejection. If the group is a large one, a rigid hierarchical structure is built from the top down, with no safeguards against the misuse of power. There is no room for personal decision making at the lower levels of the group. Errant disciples are harshly disciplined if they're suspected of disobedience. Authoritarian leaders demand total commitment and unquestioning loyalty.

Intrusion and blurred personal boundaries. Privacy is a rare commodity in a dysfunctional religious group. Members' thoughts, emotions, time, and often, financial resources are not their own. Some leaders claim to read followers' minds while others arrange intense confessional scenarios in order to get inside members' heads.

Sometimes leaders have sexual relationships with members, claiming it is part of enlightenment and communion with the Divine.

Degradation. Public and private humiliation is used to immobilize members to prevent their dissent or voluntary departure. Some dysfunctional religious groups teach that any form of positive self-regard is sin or a major impediment to spiritual growth. When members show signs of honoring their own integrity, they may be held up as bad examples, scolded, told they are possessed by devils or evil spirits, or that they are too ignorant to understand the truth the group teaches. The logic system is closed and circular, anyone who questions cannot be a true believer, so concerns don't count anyway.

Monopoly on truth. Dysfunctional religious groups often claim to own the sole way to salvation or enlightenment. If members choose not to believe part of the creed or if they display signs of individuality, they are quickly, even forcibly, brought back into the fold or they are banished. Groupthink is the rule rather than the exception. Individualistic interpretation of the teachings is considered heresy. Unsure how to apply rules to their lives, members are instructed by someone above them in the hierarchy.

Total control over members' lives. Extremely dysfunctional groups may require that members move into a group home, give all their money to the organization, and surrender the ability to make choices about how they will spend their time. Followers may be told what to wear or when they can or cannot have sex. Other groups maintain high levels of control without group living arrangements. Time commitments required for meetings may be enormous, and demands are made to give up friendships outside the group. Members are pressured, if not outright dictated to, about types of jobs they may hold, what they should eat, what they may read, and whom they may date.

Rigid institutional boundaries. The more a group isolates members from the world and the more exclusionary it is in drawing lines between its members and outsiders, the greater the potential for dysfunction. Thick boundaries and black-and-white thinking intensify group interactions. This intensity is often mistaken for spiritual energy. When outsiders are cast as enemies, most of the anger that arises in such pressure-cooker circumstances is displaced outside the group. Members begin to feel that they are the elect, the chosen, and voluntarily pull further away from the rest of the human race. In time they come

30

to depend completely on the group for the satisfaction of their social needs.

Secrecy and deception, both inside and outside the group. To fortify its boundaries, the dysfunctional religious group protects potential recruits and members from the undermining forces of reality.

One of the most popular mottoes of these groups is "We are not a religion." Potential recruits may not even be told the name or purpose of the organization until weeks after they become involved. Sometimes conflicts with outsiders are engineered and exaggerated in order to tighten cohesion within the group. When individual members exercise too much critical thinking or freedom, rumors may be started about them as a way to ensure control.

A mission or a cause. The more obsessively a group focuses on the task it has set for itself, the greater the chances for dysfunction to arise. Causes range from establishment of a church to fund-raising or recruitment. In many groups, the mission is to save members from a predicted apocalypse. When such emphasis is put on the task or the cause, there is no room for members to develop an independent frame of reference. The task enmeshes members further, and it provides a visible way for leaders to measure members' supposed spiritual progress. Advancement on the path is judged by the amount of money or the number of members brought into the organization.

Ends justify the means. Whenever a group focuses on mission instead of the spiritual needs of members, a great temptation exists to achieve the mission by any means, including lying, cheating, and stealing. These practices are accepted, even though doctrine may explicitly forbid them. When members raise an ethical question, they may be told that nothing done in the service of God can be sinful; the suspect acts in God's will; or that enlightenment has bestowed immunity to ethics and virtues. When the spiritual teacher orders members to violate their values, they often are told, as I was, that it is a paradox, a lesson to shock them out of preconceived patterns, or a test of their loyalty to the group.

Given the characteristics of dysfunctional religious groups, it is no surprise that, even if families of origin were healthy and self-esteem was relatively high, members trapped in these organizations suffer deep emotional hurts. Like people who have been sexually or physically abused, spiritually abused adults often repress the pain that comes from being betrayed by those they trusted with their souls. They become the walking wounded, codependent to the core, as though they had grown up in the most dysfunctional of families.

Those of us who did grow up in less-than-healthy families may be more easily seduced into damaging groups and have a tougher time leaving them than other people do. Even if a childhood heritage of overt religious abuse has not carried over into adult religious experiences, the trauma and unresolved shame from physical, sexual, or emotional abuse suffered as children makes people especially susceptible to exploitation in the name of God. In a misguided attempt to be loved and accepted, we may find ourselves taken in by authoritarian leaders because of a learned tendency to look to others for self-esteem and relief from psychic pain.

CHAPTER THREE

Spirituality—The Redemption Dimension

In a Hindu tale, a fierce tigress who was very pregnant hungrily stalked the edge of a high, steep cliff, her eyes on a herd of well-fed goats grazing the emerald grass of the valley below. She hesitated, but her ravenous need for meat won out, and with a great leap she sprang into the center of the herd. The goats bounded away, but the tigress lay still, her neck broken. As she died, her contractions began. With her last breath, she gave birth to a cub.

Hours later, when it seemed safe, the goats wandered back to the clearing. Kindhearted beasts, they adopted the little tiger and raised him as if he were their own offspring. Once he was weaned, they taught him to feed on grass, which kept him frail and meek. He learned to communicate by bleating. Although he was troubled by a nagging doubt that something was wrong with him, that he wasn't a very good goat, his life was calm and predictable.

Then one night, as he lay fast asleep, he was startled awake by a roar so loud it seemed to shake the hills. Immediately his goat family scattered, and only the dazed tiger remained. He knew he should run, but he was overcome with curiosity and stood unmoving as a magnificent tiger padded up to him. "Why are you here among these goats, little fellow?" the tiger growled. To the cub's amazement, he could understand the tiger language.

The old tiger picked the young one up by the scruff of his golden neck and carried him off to the jungle. Bleating, the cub squirmed in protest. Only when they came to a watering hole did the tiger stop to show him their reflection. "Can't you see, you look just like me?" demanded the old tiger. "Why are you pretending to be a goat, chewing grass and bleating?"

The two continued on to the tiger's lair, where the elder offered the cub a chunk of bloody meat left over from a previous kill. Frightened, the little tiger crouched, his ears flat against his head. When he bleated weakly, the tiger pushed the piece of meat into the young one's mouth.

This food was the best the cub had ever tasted! He ate his fill, feeling every muscle and sinew and cell of his body suffuse with energy. Arching his back, he stretched and swished his tail, delighting in the sensation. Then, quite without planning it, he threw back his head and sounded a glorious roar.

That roar of awakening—the sudden understanding of who we are beneath our conditioning and the certain knowledge of how we fit into the vast and complex fabric of the cosmos, is what the spiritual search is all about. It is the process, whether lengthy or instantaneous, of truly coming into our own. Some of us, like the tiger cub in the story, encounter a mentor or a life experience which teaches us that we can never go back to live contentedly with the goats .

For others, this first encounter with the self isn't quite so dramatic. It begins, instead, with a feeling of uneasiness, a sense that there is more to be learned outside the herd; discontentment provokes a spiritual search for the missing piece to give meaning to existence.

Once begun, this journey may be a long one. Even when one has endured the crucible of a tigerish encounter, growth rarely ends with one enormous roar of awakening. Instead, that loud "Ah hah!" serves as a starting point. Much remains to be learned before one can become a wise, old tiger. More often than not, life is punctuated with a series of insights along the way.

The Search for Answers
Who am I?
What is my purpose on earth?
Is there a God?
If so, what is my relationship to God?
What will happen when I die?

No matter what feelings or events trigger it, the search for answers to these questions is universal, as natural as breathing. In fact, the word *spirituality* comes from the root meaning "to blow" or "to breathe." When people begin to examine sacred issues, they move more closely to the meaning of life and to spirit. Although this quest for understanding is an individual one, it often draws people into religious groups and organized doctrine. After all, philosophers and theologians have tried to come up with answers for millennia. An exploration of others' solutions to cosmic dilemmas hones one's own understanding. Every system of teaching offers a slightly different answer to life's big questions. Sometimes these solutions to existential dilemmas conflict with one another. Some of the doctrines may conflict with one's own deeply held sense of what is true. So the search is typically bewildering, with many twists and turns.

Moments of Truth

Existential questions arise as children move into adolescence. It is then that they begin to define themselves apart from their parents. Suddenly they scrutinize their religious upbringing. Although dogmas, rituals, and membership in a particular religion may be handed down from parents, spirituality (the faith of fathers and mothers) cannot be passed on as a legacy. Each person must find his or her own truth. Sometimes that means examining and testing the religious teachings learned as children. At other times it means moving beyond families' belief systems.

Tracy, who was raised in an Italian Catholic family in Maryland, considered herself a true believer until high school. Then, all of a sudden, catechism didn't make sense anymore. "I was walking to my eleventh-grade English class and somebody asked me my opinion about something," she recalls. "For some reason the question really penetrated. I realized that I had no opinions of my own because I'd never really thought about anything. I'd just learned stuff and believed it. The only thing I could do was to regurgitate what I'd been taught. That realization was my first contact with self."

That moment of truth caused Tracy to scrutinize everything she had learned about her religion, and eventually she rejected the Church. She received a scholarship to a distant Catholic women's college and a year later transferred to a state university. There she joined a small study group that followed the teachings of Gurdjieff, a Russian mystic who synthesized Eastern and Western esoteric teachings earlier in this century. For a time, Tracy found her reading and meditation to be liberating, but doubts began to creep in. She explains, "Gurdjieff believed that the moon is a very strong controlling factor in people's lives, and I just couldn't buy it, so I dropped out of the group, but I decided to go on investigating other teachings.

She tried Transcendental Meditation next. "I paid my 25 dollars, received my mantra, meditated my little heart out, and ate brown rice," Tracy remembers. "It was definitely worthwhile and I got something out of it, but it didn't fulfill my desire for knowledge. I had so many questions, and there was no mechanism to get the answers I needed. I was looking for a guru." Tracy's search for a spiritual master took her to San Francisco, where she studied with a yoga teacher for three months, but still she remained unsatisfied. Not until several months later did she discover what she believed would be the ultimate answer to her search— Scientology. It was an answer that turned out to be painful, as well.

Like Tracy, we test out frameworks of belief and reject them, discover new systems, live with them for a time, and then move on when the answers no longer fit. Sometimes it seems that the more questions we have answered, the more questions arise. In the midst of the confusing process of shaping our beliefs, sometimes we want somebody to tell us the right answer.

Since religions are social institutions whose members reflect their central beliefs, the move beyond holy books and into the church or temple shows that each group has a unique culture. Some fit us even though we can't believe the dogmas. Other religious groups leave us cold, even though we may see wisdom in their teachings. When we discover the group we have joined is not right for us, we have a clearer picture of who we are. At least we know what we don't believe.

Grappling with the ambiguities and paradoxes of life can be frightening and lonely. Even if we're committed to individual seeking, we often need to be with others who share our spiritual goals. A body of believers provides not only companionship along the path, but also support and guidance to deal with everyday life and achieve personal fulfillment. The old saying that there is safety in numbers can be true. In the case of dysfunctional religious groups, however, it is decidedly false. People who join dysfunctional religious groups or cults don't ask to be spiritually abused. They set out to seek the truth—just like the rest of us.

Times of Transition

An emotional crisis may spark a spiritual journey that impels some people into a religious group. This crisis may be hitting bottom in an addiction, losing a loved one, or re-evaluating priorities. At no stage of life are people immune to hurt and emotional upheaval. In the struggle to make sense of a crisis, people often realize that they simply cannot go on alone. At these times they may feel extremely disconnected from God. They want to surrender to a Higher Power but are unsure if they can develop a working relationship with the Divine without having the mediation of a religious group.

At age 28, Anna was divorced, had two small children, and was almost ready to graduate from college. Even though she was romantically involved with a man she considered perfect, she had no idea what to do with her life, and she felt she needed something more. "My longing had nothing to do with anyone other than me. I remember sitting in the bedroom alone and saying, 'I don't know what's happening to me, but I want to know whether this hunger has anything to do with God.' Then the veil parted and I knew I had to take my children and find an apartment of my own."

Two hours later and two blocks away, Anna found her apartment, but her crisis continued. Life did not make sense to her any longer. Her new apartment manager, a member of the Holy Order of Mans, a Christian group that loosely followed the teachings of Saint Paul, suggested that Anna seek counseling from the group.

Anna went. She learned that *Mans* originated from an acronym meaning "order within mankind." The worldwide group of 5,000 members was composed of a hierarchy of brothers and sisters, reverends, priests, brother teachers, and master teachers. The fifty-member local chapter conducted missions on the streets wearing habits and friars' robes. "The Holy Order of Mans taught eclectically—the law of love, the law of prayer, cause and effect, and the Bible," says Anna. "They held Masses, communion, and baptisms. Most important for me was the spiral staircase of spiritual growth. The staircase spirals upward and returns you again and again to the same lessons until you learn them."

Once Anna began interacting with other people in the group, her spiritual growth accelerated. "In a group, the energy level is much higher," she explains. "I could feel it physically. I experienced a real spiritual and emotional awakening."

Social Solutions

Sometimes idealism and complex social problems drive spiritual seekers to explore alternative religions. Conventional political solutions to problems like poverty and hunger, global conflicts, and racism do not seem to work. So the discontented seek out a religious group they believe can change the world and transform themselves.

Gary was a member of the Divine Light Mission for more than seven years. He lived in the group's ashram for two years, beginning when he was a college junior in 1972. His connection was the result of an unfocused spiritual search. In high school he had been involved in many social organizations with religious ties. Raised a Presbyterian, he was excited by the new brand of radical Christianity even though some aspects seemed like a step backward on the spiritual path. "I was excited by the novelty and the commitment. But when they got into a very intolerant, fundamentalist mind-set, I was less attracted," he explains.

Next, student activism appealed to his idealism, but he felt that since the sixties, the political scene had devolved into learning how to hate properly. The war was winding down, and the protest movement was tapering off. Gary was interested in something else.

He first learned of the Divine Light Mission through his roommate. Gary says, "The theology of it seemed to mesh with what I already believed. It was almost universally individualistic. I was told that throughout time there have been great spiritual masters like Jesus, Buddha, and Krishna. Now there's this one. It wasn't intolerant of other religions and didn't deny their validity." It sounded good to him, so he began attending meetings.

Full Circle

Some of us begin a spiritual search without realizing that's what we are doing. At first we look for intellectual and philosophical answers or emotional healing; only later do we understand that the nourishment we seek is for our souls rather than our minds. Occasionally, after we have wandered for years through complex twists and turns and taken innumerable side trips, we wind up back where we began. Even so, the journey has been necessary because we have changed. The process and encounters along the way teach us the lessons we need to learn. Often they bring wisdom.

We are like the man in the story recorded in commentaries on the Talmud. He believed that if he wandered from place to place and begged for food he would become more holy. He arrived at a town where people worshipped idols, and asked, "Why do you worship statues?"

A pagan replied, "So they will provide me with food."

The wanderer responded, "How can you be such an idiot? This idol can't provide anything. It is made from stone and doesn't even have the power to move from where it sits!"

Replied the idol worshipper, "Whom do you serve?"

The aesthetic answered, "I serve the God whose might prevails throughout the universe, the God who cares for and feeds all of his creatures everywhere."

"You expect me to believe that?" the idol worshipper scoffed. "If this god you serve is everywhere, then why did you leave your home to look for him? If he feeds everyone, why do you wander around and beg for food?" He returned to his prostrations. The seeker knew the pagan was right and returned to his homeland.

Brenda, whose spiritual journey seems to be taking her full circle, was raised Lutheran in a severely dysfunctional family setting. At age 11 she became an atheist. "I went through communion with my fingers crossed because my mother wouldn't let me back out of being confirmed," she says. She has been involved with groups she calls cults since she was a teenager. At 38, she reflects on a convoluted spiritual journey and says she is grateful for her traditional religious background. "I wouldn't be surprised if someday, somehow, I came out a Lutheran again," she says. "Not because it's better, but, at my mother's funeral a few years ago, the traditional forms and rituals from my childhood meant a lot to me." She's still put off, however, by the focus on church basketball games and the soup kitchen, rather than the more mystical direction her life is headed.

Brenda's first "cult" involvement came not through a religious organization, but through a group of intellectuals. "One characteristic of a cult is an exclusive path to salvation," she explains. "This group of thinkers believed the world was intellectually dormant and were going to start creating ideas again."

While she maintained her involvement with the intellectuals, much to their dismay, she joined Scientology and kept a dual allegiance for the next four years. Four hours a night, five nights a week, she took Scientology classes, and on the sixth night she went to parties with her classmates. She also attended college, majoring in medieval history and was deeply involved in her classes.

Eventually the coffeehouse philosophers disbanded and the Scientologists asked her to leave the group. "The ethics officer unofficially kicked me out because I was mixing technology," she says. "I worked as an activity director in a nursing home. I used reality therapy, a technique to help the senile orient themselves using colors and big clocks on the wall. My work did not disagree with anything in Scientology, but I was ordered out anyway." Her dismissal from the group was so disillusioning that she ceased contact with friends still involved with the organization.

Even so, after her departure, she continued to apply many of the principles she had learned in the group to her daily life while attending meetings of a Wiccan coven at the invitation of a friend. "It was similar to any other church service except you did not wear clothes," Brenda explained. "I mean, after you got past the nudity, there really was not much difference between the Wiccan coven and most other religions. The people were not evil or cruel. They had a lot of teas, recipes, and rituals that I didn't feel drawn to. I phased out because I was not challenged or interested."

Still seeking but remaining a disbeliever in God, she followed another friend into a spiritual psychotherapy group that combined Sufism and work on childhood issues. Finally Brenda had found an organization where she belonged. "I was involved with that for five years and it really was my life. Scientology had been a very passionate interest, but I would call the Sufi group my life. I was defined by that group."

Addiction: A Thirst for Spirit

The act of consciously healing from addictions or dysfunctional family issues can bring spiritual growth. Although we may begin by trying to assimilate other people's beliefs, eventually we listen to the voice within. The spiritual path of dependency and healing from dependency can be powerful. Self-defeating behavior and its subsequent healing mirrors the fall and redemption theme of Christianity and shamanic traditions. Many experience for the first time this redemption in a Twelve Step program where the need for a relationship with the sacred is affirmed. Weekly meetings and the Twelve Step program challenge us spiritually and help us find God personally.

John, a recovering drug and sex addict, says, "None of us suffers from just one compulsion. I'm recovering from obsessive compulsive behavior." His spiritual life has always been important to him—before, during, and after his experience with the Unification Church. He has discovered a strong link between his past substance abuse and his longing for the sacred. "People are starved for a relationship with God, and that's why there's such a problem with substance abuse and sexual addiction," he says. "We're starving for some kind of spiritual nourishment, and we don't know how to get it. So we use alcohol and other drugs or have sex to quench that thirst. But it's a spiritual thirst, and feeding it physically doesn't work."

Well into healing from his addictions, John says, "In recovery my spiritual process is more individual and private than in the Unification Church. I can develop it in my own way and at my own pace. It is important to have a connection with my Higher Power that is unique, personal, and private."

A Nation of Seekers

This urge to foster a unique, personal, and private connection with God is reflected in American society. While church membership continues to decline, groups that offer more mystical, individual experiences continue to grow. Transplanted Eastern religions, new religions, and charismatic renewal Christianity are on the upswing.

Sacred myth, too, has experienced a surge of renewed interest as underscored by the popularity of Joseph Campbell's books and videos. Myth, more than mere storytelling or fantasy, is a metaphor for a deeper, more spiritual concern. Aspects of the New Age movement have struck a chord in millions of people across the country. Suddenly in religious bookstores, the writings of the mystics—the Desert Fathers, St. Teresa of Avila, Meister Eckhart, Julian of Norwich—have been moved from the back shelves to more prominent locations. At Twelve Step meetings, the talk in scattered small groups after coffee these days is about meditation, yoga, and spiritual retreats.

Despite surface appearances and the decline of mainstream religious institutions, a strong spiritual undercurrent exists in our culture that is often unrecognized. We are a nation of individualistic spiritual seekers. According to a 1986 Gallup Poll, 94 percent of all Americans believe in God or in a universal spirit. This number has remained relatively consistent since 1952. Eighty-four percent believe that God is a Heavenly Father. Only 7 percent see the Divine as an abstract idea or an impersonal creator.

Most Americans say having a personal relationship with God influences the way people live their lives. Eight out of ten who think of God as a Heavenly Father believe that He guides them in making decisions. More than half believe God speaks to them. Almost nine out of ten people who believe in God also believe in miracles.

According to a recent readership survey conducted by *Better Homes and Gardens* magazine, most people feel closest to God through prayer and meditation. Other common catalysts for deepening one's relationship to the Creator are times of crisis, joy, and religious services. More than half believe that it is possible to be spiritual without being religious, and more than one-third complain that organized religions don't meet people's spiritual needs.

With such a strong emphasis on individual spirituality, it is no wonder that organized religion may not satisfy. While forty years ago, the Gallup Poll found that three-fourths of the people in the United States felt that organized religion was important, today only 55 percent think so. Fewer than four out of ten Americans attend church on a weekly basis.

Sociologists believe that this wide-scale rejection of the faith of our fathers and mothers is a result of social upheaval. During the last few decades the United States became a more mobile society. Today few of us live near the churches our parents attend. The assassinations of John F. Kennedy, Martin Luther King Jr., Malcolm X, and Robert Kennedy, the Vietnam War, drug abuse, and the social changes of the sixties created a generation of idealists dissatisfied with the existing social institutions, including families and churches.

Signs of upheaval are all around us. Ultraconservative religious groups decry the move away from institutionalized belief as a satanically inspired plot to destroy the country. Many adherents of New Age beliefs are certain that these people are unenlightened Neanderthals. Some cult experts claim that Eastern and new religions offer only pain and enslavement. Many people who belong to new and Eastern groups compare deprogrammers to fascists. Some psychologists label all mystical experiences as hallucinations and the thirst for spirit as neurosis. The mystics disagree. Many scientists who formerly cringed at the mention of God now see evidence of the Divine in the new physics and chaos theory.

This bewilderment over the "proper" way to approach the sacred is nothing new. A story recorded by the Sufi poet Rumi in the thirteenth century lends insight into the spiritual choices we face now and the eagerness of others to dictate the path we should follow. In Rumi's story, a shepherd spent his time in the fields with his sheep, talking to God. "Dearest One," he crooned, "I want to give you goat's milk when You are thirsty. I want to comb Your hair to get the tangles out and rub Your feet when they ache. Let me sweep and tidy Your room, wash Your clothes, and tuck You into bed every night when it's time for You to sleep."

Moses, the lawgiver, was passing by. Curious at what he overheard, he stopped and asked the shepherd, "You there, who are you speaking with?"

"Why, God, of course," stammered the shepherd.

"This is a terrible sin!" stormed Moses. "You cannot talk with God about milk and dirty clothes. It is blasphemy. And you cannot address Him in that familiar tone of voice. He is magnificent and should be addressed with fear and awe."

Ashamed, the shepherd tore his clothes and went out into the desert to repent the terrible thing he had done.

Moses continued along his way, a smug smile on his face until he saw a flash of lightning and heard the booming voice of God. "What have you done?" God asked.

"I've pointed out that ignorant shepherd's errors and caused him to mend his ways," Moses replied with the slightest trace of pride.

"You have separated one of mine from me," chided God. "Everyone worships me in a different way. There is no better or worse way to do it, since all perceive me in their own way, given their understanding. I don't look at the words people say or the rituals they perform. I look into my children's hearts."

The spiritual journey is ultimately an interior one that takes place in the hearts. We all begin the quest from a different place, and the direction we take is profoundly affected by our emotional makeup and our personal history. When we wake up to the multilayered motivations that inspire us to choose one path over another—even a path that may impede our journey—we are better able to make wise choices and to tolerate the choices of others.

CHAPTER FOUR

Unholy Ghosts—The Effect of Childhood Spiritual Wounds on Adult Choices

Childhood experiences involving spiritual abuse leave people vulnerable to exploitation by dysfunctional religious groups as adults. Physical, emotional, or sexual abuse also have the power to leave debilitating spiritual scars. Growing up in a dysfunctional family can damage the ability to trust and undermine self-worth. The role religion and spirituality play in a survivor's life can be altered dramatically.

Abuse and shame make people feel fragmented, inherently flawed, hopeless, and unlovable. It is difficult, with such feelings, to conceive of a loving God. As a result, groups or individuals who promise hope, unconditional love, or relief of childhood emotional pain, or who fill the overwhelming emptiness find the wounded and self-loathing easy targets.

Suffer the Little Children

On the wall of my Sunday school classroom hung a picture of Jesus that fascinated me. He smiled as handsome, well-scrubbed children pressed toward Him, vying for a place on His lap. "Suffer the little children to come unto me," read the caption engraved in brass on the frame. Jesus' hand was raised, and I couldn't figure out whether he meant to bless the children or slap them. It frightened me to think that the Son of God might hurt the children in the picture—children who were obviously better than me. If He wanted them to suffer, what did He have planned for me? Only in junior high school did I discover that *suffer* in King James English meant *allow*.

Some people grow up to believe that God endorses suffering and punishment. When childhood religious experiences are frightening, God is pictured as punitive and dictatorial. Even though He seems to smile on us, we can't help but wonder if His benign expression is a tricky mask to lure us onto His lap so he can surprise us with a cosmic smack on the head.

Children raised in strict religious homes may be subjected to disciplinary techniques that cross the line from guilt to shame. Children who misbehave may be called sinners and be told that their actions displeased not only their parents, but God as well. They are assured of eternal damnation, sometimes for simply acting in age-appropriate ways. Shame, fear, and constant vigilance become bound up with spirituality. Since these overwhelmingly awful feelings have to do with identities rather than actions, they come to live in terror of God's wrath for acts of misbehavior.

Even parents who are not strictly religious sometimes use religiously based, guilt-provoking tactics to shape their children's behavior. Jewish children who resist attending temple or Hebrew school hear detailed stories about the Holocaust. Christian children who refuse to eat their vegetables are told they are breaking Jesus' heart or causing starvation among children in Third World nations. Whether religion is used for shaming at home or in a formal religious setting, early, punitive encounters with a Higher Power may shape images of the Divine in adult life.

For more than twenty years, Susan tried to heal her deep spiritual scars. She was raised in the Plymouth Brethren, a small Protestant sect. Although her father left the sect, her aunts, uncles, and grandfather adhered to the rigid doctrines. "You couldn't do anything except sit, take a walk, or read the Bible on Sunday. At home, I was allowed to listen to rock-and-roll music and wear makeup, but everyplace else taught me that these things were wrong."

To compensate for the absence of Susan's wayward father, her relatives insisted that she attend a conservative religious summer camp in upstate New York, beginning at age 10.

"The summer I was 13, about 500 of us were jammed into a pavilion. The minister screamed at us while he held up huge pictures of liquor bottles. He told us we would go to hell if we drank or danced. I felt convicted of my sin, because even if I hadn't done those things, I planned to. If he mentioned God's love, I don't remember it."

The teenagers were ordered to bow their heads and raise their hands if they wanted to accept Jesus Christ as their savior and be forgiven. Susan raised her hand. The minister told the teenagers to stand and come forward. Susan and several others approached the altar. At the end of the service, three camp counselors surrounded her. "They tried to make me confess to certain sins and accept Jesus," Susan says. "They led me in prayer. I said things I wasn't sure of. I was reduced to hysteria."

After weeks of daily Bible study, Susan was pressured to witness in front of the entire camp. "I'm introverted and I was mortified. I didn't want to tell them what a rotten person I was," she says. "Besides, I wasn't sure what had happened to me, so I postponed it. Finally my counselor told me, 'If you don't do this, you'll lose your salvation.' My counselor quoted scripture, and I believed it. Somehow, I managed to get up and mutter something so I wouldn't lose my salvation."

The summer camps left Susan with a legacy of shame she has carried throughout her life. Despite brief periods of independent thinking, she spent many years in repressive religious organizations. Only at age 40 did she find the courage to break free from her trap of fearful unworthiness and deal with the emotional and spiritual abuse of her childhood.

A Legacy of Shame

Some parents feel they fail to live up to their religious potential. Their shame may intensify their demands on their children to fit into the religious system of their choice. In a sense, they expect their children to atone for their sins. Susan's father may have been aware of what occurred at the summer camps, but he still insisted she attend. He felt compelled not to jeopardize his daughter's salvation.

Shame-filled parents send strong messages of approval when their children attain piety and devotion. Al, whose mother had once been in a convent, never knew the details of her leaving the order. He guessed it had something to do with expressing her sexuality. Despite her silence, Al took on her heavy burden of shame. He reacted by becoming a compliant student in the parochial schools he attended. Twenty-five years later, in psychotherapy, he has started to recall repressed memories about his school days.

In fifth grade, a priest showed Al's class a filmstrip about the Maryknoll Brotherhood's mission in South America. He then passed out cards asking students to make a commitment to life in a religious order. Al wrote that he wanted to become a brother and was told to show his card to his parents before mailing it in. "My mother was thrilled. She thought she was going to be saved for her sin of having kids instead of staying in the convent. My being a brother would compensate." he says. "My dad thought it was pretty cool that I was going to do that for my mom."

After elementary school, Al attended a Catholic high school for boys, but in college he completely rejected Catholicism. Today when he discusses his family's religious heritage, his voice becomes strident. "The die-hard Roman Catholic believes that anything else is a perversion not only of Christianity, but of religion. I remain convinced that the Catholic approach to child-rearing and adolescent education, especially in sexual ethics and behavior, is really warped. Masturbating can earn you a ticket straight to hell if you don't have time to say a sincere act of contrition." Even though he turned away from his faith, he clung tightly to his eagerness to please. After graduation, he followed his wife into The Way International, a fundamentalist Protestant sect he is convinced destroyed his family. His fifteen-year involvement ended only two years ago.

When our religious experiences as children are negative, we may feel compelled, like Al, to escape into atheism. Instinctively we run from the abusive religious experiences of childhood instead of moving toward a well-considered philosophy. But if we do not resolve the psychological issues underlying our antireligion stance, our cynical exteriors are only facades. We still ache for someone or something outside ourselves to meet our emotional needs and fill our spiritual emptiness. Like Al, we may find ourselves pulled into a system as repressive as the family faith we escaped.

A Family Theology of Abuse

Some parents use the Bible's "Spare the rod and spoil the child" dictum to justify physical abuse. Beatings, they reason, are sanctioned by God. If spared physical abuse, children from rigidly religious homes may be told they are sinners or are evil. Children growing up in this negative and condemning atmosphere often develop an image of a rageful God who sanctions the abuse they receive.

Even when religious abuse in the home isn't blatant, it can still be a major factor in adult views of spirituality. Some families' fear of God isn't used selectively as a punishment but takes on the dimensions of a family curse. God's will is the direct cause of misfortunes ranging from divorce and financial problems to substance abuse. Bad things happen as Divine punishment or to provide a cosmic lesson. When parents adhere to this theology, they use religion to avoid fully acknowledging family problems or seeking solutions. Learned helplessness becomes a virtue by taking on the religious gloss of pious endurance and devoted passivity. To question, complain, or take action is to defy the Creator. People schooled in this way find the pattern difficult to break.

Renee, formerly a nun, grew up in a chaotic family that blamed God for the misery her family suffered. Paradoxically, when she fled her home, religion became her refuge and escape. "Home was a frightening place," she says. "My father was an alcoholic and had multiple sclerosis, which added a lot of anger to his alcoholism. My mother was codependent. The drama revolved around my parents, with the rest of us standing on the sidelines. The only place I found order and consistent rewards for my behavior was in parochial school."

In school she remembers some severe physical and emotional punishment meted out by the nuns, mainly to the little boys. Renee experienced no harsh treatment. "I was a good girl and I was rewarded for that, so I felt secure," she says. "I loved to go to school because it was peaceful."

Eventually, Renee's father's violence increased, and he was placed periodically in nursing homes. Her mother focused exclusively on him, ignoring Renee and her siblings, forcing them to fend for themselves. She rationalized her neglect in religious terms. Renee explains, "My mother told us that God had given her a sick husband so she would care for him and God would care for us kids. I felt angry that God was taking care of us. Where was Mom? I wanted her to leave my father or kill him to get him out of our lives."

Her wish that her parents would divorce stood in direct conflict to the Catholic belief that vows made before God cannot be broken under any circumstances. It was a conviction that kept her in the convent long after serious doubts began to surface. Because of the solace she had found in parochial school, entering the convent at age 18 seemed a logical plan. It also pleased her family. "To give your child to God was honorable," she explains. "The convent seemed to provide the education, guidance, and sanity I wanted. My father never provided anything; so I was looking for dear old Dad to tell me how to live. I wanted to float around in a habit and know exactly what to do and how to do it."

Existential Emptiness

Spiritual abuse is not the only cause of shame in a family. Incest, battery, and emotional abuse also leave family members reeling with feelings of unworthiness. Everyone who grows up in an abusive family has been spiritually wounded. One's sense of not being good enough extends well beyond the psychological realm into the spiritual one; after all, being tarnished to the core is what the story of Adam and Eve is all about. Whether we believe we're cut off from God or from other human beings because of our sinful natures, we feel helpless and hopeless. We feel doomed or damned, even if we were raised in an atheistic or agnostic setting.

Shame is not a feeling we are born with. It is a learned response, and in very small doses it serves a useful purpose. Researchers have discovered that human beings do not feel unworthy and unlovable until they reach the age of 18 months, when they are ready to develop an identity separate from that of their parents. Painful as the expulsion from the paradise of infancy may be, it is part of growing up. When we learn that certain things we do cause our parents to appear not to love us, we feel humiliated and unworthy. Then we are forgiven and the interpersonal bonds are restored, leaving us humbler and wiser.

In abusive or dysfunctional families, shaming is not a short or isolated incident, because love is conditional. It is a scarce resource. When children transgress by breaking family rules, unspoken or otherwise, they are not forgiven but are treated like outcasts. Forgiveness, if it is granted, is unpredictable and usually has little to do with what one says or does. When children are raised without validation and unconditional love, their shame grows until it typifies their lives.

Shame can paralyze us and make us feel so flawed that we question our right to exist. As author John Bradshaw puts it, we have holes in our souls. Although we grow taller, psychologically and spiritually we remain contracted and empty. Shame becomes an emptiness inside that drives our search for meaning. Too terrified to find our own answers, we may look to a group for validation. Without approval and reassurance as adults, we may feel we don't count.

To complicate matters, childhood trauma prepares sufferers to cope with adult realities in unhealthy ways. Emotional, physical, or sexual abuse makes them terrified to assert themselves, even in dangerous situations. As children, they had to submit to the total power of adults in their lives. Complete compliance is a common way most abused children survive. Rebellion, on the other hand, might be life threatening.

Brenda's father died when she was 2 years old, a few days before her mother gave birth to a younger brother. After the funeral, the extended family walked away from the young widow and her children for good. Consumed with grief and unable to cope, Brenda's mother left the little girl for long periods with a baby-sitter who beat and sexually molested Brenda.

Except for adolescence, when she became an agnostic, Brenda sought spiritual answers to the questions her father's death triggered: Why had she been abandoned? Why had she suffered such abuse? She began her search at a very early age. "My first memories are of God," she says. "If I had not lost everything when I was 2, I probably would not have wondered about the existence of God when I was 3 or 4. Four-year-olds are not supposed to worry about God. I knew the major philosophical arguments for the existence of God before I was 8 because I wondered about Him so much."

Although childhood abuse set her on a spiritual path, it also stripped her of emotional strength and a clear sense of self to allow her to shed her victim role. She remembers an incident of near-paralysis that happened before her involvement with organized religion began. "This therapist decided that if he could get me to scream I would be fine, so he sat on my chest. I couldn't breathe, I remember not struggling and then losing consciousness. I thought I was about to die, but I didn't tell him to get off my chest. As a child I had learned that if a sadist is feeding off your pain and you show discomfort, she will do something to make it worse. In the presence of an enemy, I acted as though nothing was happening. My therapist taught me that I would let myself die rather than stand up for myself. That's the psychological baggage I carry."

Seeds of Religious Addiction

Childhood abuse leaves us with existential emptiness and few healthy coping skills. The wounds also may draw us into religious addiction. Religion, like a drug, can dull pain and encourage relationships that may feel passionate and alive. The group beliefs become our salvation, our security blanket, our defense against the real world and against our own pain.

Crystal, an incest victim, was raised by an alcoholic father who married seven times. When she was 5, he left her mother, also an alcoholic, and fled with the children, first to Texas, then to Arkansas. "I took on the mother role at 5 or 6 years old," she says. "I remember standing on a chair, doing dishes and ironing. I remember standing behind the door and crying with blood in my panties at 5." When she tried to resist sexual abuse, her father accused her of being possessed." He said the bed jumped up and down when I was born and that I was born with a veil over my face, so I belonged to the devil. All that stuff about evil spirits terrified me."

At 15, Crystal considered suicide. But she reconsidered, and at 18 she married and had a child. Making her husband the center of her life helped to remove her emotional hurt. Soon afterward, pregnant with her second child, she saw her spouse kiss another woman at a Christmas party. "I was depressed from the hormonal changes of pregnancy and I felt very confused and unloved. But I wasn't able to talk to my husband about it," she explains.

The next day Crystal went to church and was handed a tract that outlined the steps to salvation. "I accepted Jesus Christ as my personal savior, and my life changed completely," she recalls. "Because I needed love and was unable to ask for it, I got lost in the charismatic movement. I went to meetings every night, sometimes twice a day. Church gave me an emotional high, security, everything. Before, my husband was my god, and when he abandoned me I found a substitute to replace him."

Some people who grow up in dysfunctional families learn as adults to medicate emotional pain with alcohol and other drugs. For a while, this seems to induce a chemical state of grace. When shame returns, they exorcise it with another drink or another pill. Soon, however, no matter how many chemicals are ingested, dissatisfaction and the aching spiritual emptiness remain.

When addicts finally hit bottom, they may switch addictions by taking shelter in a religious organization without working on core issues such as abuse and shame. As transformative as religion can be, it is not recovery. Unless a person deals with the psychological demons that lead to alcohol and other drug use, in therapy or in a Twelve Step program, sobriety is temporary.

John, who grew up in a small West Texas town in the heart of the Bible Belt, tells of his destructive involvement in the Unification Church. Although his grandmother was a devout member of the fundamentalist Church of Christ, his mother was not. Her five marriages, all to alcoholics, left little room in her life for religion or for her son. John never knew his father, who had been killed in a car accident rumored to be alcohol related.

When John reached adolescence, he began using LSD. "In high school I did acid daily for a while," he recalls. "I never had any bad experiences with it; it was very spiritual. It opened me up and then I read people like Alan Watts and the Baba Ram Dass book *Be Here Now*."

Although high school did not interest John and he felt suffocated by his small-town environment, he graduated to please his mother. "Because my brother and sister hadn't finished school, I wanted to make her happy. Being raised in an alcoholic family, I felt my role was to make things right."

During college, 700 miles from home, he continued his drug use, drank heavily, and began to explore his sexuality. Eventually he openly declared himself gay. After two years of school, he quit to work in a Dallas restaurant. There he met a man who invited him to San Francisco, where they continued to drift aimlessly. "I was living with this guy, Jimmy. I didn't have a job. I was drinking vodka out of a bottle on Polk Street, hair down my back, overalls, the whole scene. I had twenty-five cents and a cigarette to my name when I met a girl from the church on Fisherman's Wharf. She invited me to dinner and all I cared about was getting a meal. I smoked my last cigarette on the way there."

The Unification Church, John soon discovered, was headed by True Parents, Reverend Sun Myung Moon and his wife, whom believers claimed were the two most perfected human beings in the entire world.

John believed he had found his ideal family. He immediately moved to the group's farm in northern California, stopped drinking and using, and, with the group's approval, disowned his mother and step-dad. He thought it was a child's dream come true, to be cared for, loved unconditionally, and, if he followed the rules, to be able to stay in this newfound paradise forever.

CHAPTER FIVE

The Transcendence Trap

According to a Middle Eastern parable, a country fool on a journey came to a huge city teeming with people. Never before had he seen such crowds, and soon he became confused and roamed the streets, wide-eyed. Finally, tired beyond endurance, he found a quiet spot to nap. There a problem occurred to him: When he awoke, how would he tell himself apart from the thousands of other people milling about in the streets? Fortunately, he hit upon a solution. He would tie a gourd to his left ankle so he could be absolutely certain of his own identity.

A young boy passing by spied the sleeping man and decided to play a joke on him. Carefully he removed the gourd and fastened it to his own ankle. Then he sat down to wait for the man to rouse himself. When the fool finally opened his eyes, he panicked. "If you are me," he cried, his voice trembling, "then for God's sake, who am I?"

Nobody deliberately sets out to join a dysfunctional religious group. But if unable to define self or to set boundaries, one's reality, like the fool's, is easily manipulated. For those who cannot believe in themselves, involvement with any religious group can become an addiction that leads to more confusion and pain than before they began the search for identity.

Everyone starts the spiritual adventure in ignorance. If one were already wise, the journey wouldn't be necessary. Although we believe spiritual growth to be the purpose, we often are led to groups by hidden needs and motivators. Perhaps we join religious groups for security or companionship, for easy answers or a sense of superiority. A need for approval, nurturing, unconditional love, and self-esteem can be our hidden reasons as well. Or we may be seeking ways to change society and the world. When we don't clearly understand what we need, dysfunctional groups are able to exert an irresistible pull on us.

Healthy Versus Unhealthy Seeking

A central theme running through both Eastern and Western religious traditions is the need to become childlike and drop adult defenses before salvation or enlightenment can be attained. In Matthew 18:3, Jesus instructs, "Verily, I say unto you, except ye be converted and become as little children, ye shall not enter the kingdom of heaven." The Taoist philosopher Chuang Tzu advised, "It is the child that sees the primordial secret in Nature and it is the child of ourselves we return to. The child within is simple and daring enough to live the Secret."

The childlike qualities of innocence, willingness to learn, and authenticity are prerequisites for growth. To mature spiritually, people must first remove defensive masks and allow their inner child or true self to emerge. A socially conditioned, grown-up frame of reference leaves them too jaded for spiritual work.

No matter what spiritual path is chosen, the seeker is transformed along the journey. To grow spiritually requires giving birth to oneself at the deepest level. This painful spiritual rebirth often triggers emotional regression. Even people who grew up in functional families may confuse the urge to connect with the Divine with a desire to merge with a caretaker. They want to retreat to an Eden-like state when they felt at one with their parents and were totally shameless. Seekers may come to regard a minister or spiritual teacher as a substitute parent and other members of the religious group as siblings. For a time, they may even regress into negative childish attitudes and behavior.

Because they have a solid psychological base, people who grew up in healthy families usually pass through this phase of emotional dependency fairly quickly, especially if they find a teacher or a system that serves as a spiritual coach and fosters an independent relationship to the Higher Power. Once they've found their true self, they are ready to move ahead and begin the process of spiritual unfolding.

If they connect with a spiritual teacher or leader who demands continued dependency, people with a healthy sense of self and clear boundaries will eventually decide that the group does not meet their needs and leave to find a healthier method of spiritual growth.

Adults who suffered childhood abuse or grew up in severely dysfunctional families may secretly yearn for the nurturing, loving family that never existed. If they could find this fantasy family, envisioned and embellished for years, they believe everything that is wrong would be miraculously made right. They are convinced that a group or guru can fill the existential void and remove the toxic shame. Fusing with a group causes any sense of identity to be lost.

If we are ravenous for reparenting, we may be drawn to reenact our childhoods in an attempt to complete past unfinished business. Because our wounded inner child remains emotionally frozen at the stage when the childhood trauma occurred, our efforts can be destructive and self-defeating.

No matter what dysfunction characterized the family of origin, adult children often feel compelled to repeat the past in an attempt to get it right. We may find ourselves automatically drawn to irresolvable conflicts in the office with a boss who acts like our mother or father. If one of our parents was an alcoholic, we may marry an alcoholic. If we were sexually abused as children, we may marry a sex addict. We are not gluttons for punishment, but until we come to terms with our underlying issues, we reconstruct our childhoods in an attempt to live them over again with a different outcome.

Spiritual groups provide an especially tempting setting for the reenactment of childhood trauma. When authority figures are called *father* and *mother*, and fellow believers are termed *brothers* and *sisters*, it's hard not to associate these people with childhood roles. When Anna was a toddler, she suffered a serious, disabling accident. A prolonged series of operations allowed her to reenter mainstream life in late childhood. Her early years were spent in physical pain and isolation, cut off from school, friends, and most other childhood experiences. This start in life was made even more difficult by a cold and harshly critical father whose love and attention she sought desperately but never earned.

As an adult, she formed a relationship with a spiritual teacher in the Holy Order of Mans and became totally dependent on her to validate her existence and take away the invisibility she had felt since childhood. "I was desperate," Anna says. "My teacher took a special interest in me as a student; therefore, some people in the group resented me. I was so lacking in self-confidence that when the teacher was out of town, I would sit in her chair and feel her presence so I would be motivated to go to school or work or to do anything. She became my mother, and her husband became my father. The psychological split inside me was so deep, I would probably be dead today if I had not experienced that nurturing and understanding."

Anna was fortunate. Unless our minister, teacher, or guru understands the fragility of our wounded inner child and how it differs from the childlike part of people raised in healthy families, we can expect major trouble. Enmeshed in dangerous psychodrama, we are vulnerable to betrayal and wounding at the deepest level. If our religious teacher denies or discounts our very real psychological wounds, abuse can be compounded.

The less able we are to meet our own needs, the more likely we are to look outside ourselves for people, substances, and groups to meet them for us. The more desperate we are for security, nurturing, validation, and praise, the less able we are to discriminate between those who can help us and those who will harm us. We look for love in all the wrong places, and even when we know we're being violated, we may persist. Our sense of shame makes us fear that there will never be another opportunity for spiritual growth.

The Codependency Factor

People who grew up in dysfunctional families—whether their parents were substance abusers, shopaholics, rageaholics, workaholics, or physical, sexual, or emotional abusers—possess a cluster of symptoms called codependency. These symptoms range from low self-esteem and lack of emotional balance to perfectionism, denial, communication problems, and difficulties with emotional intimacy. The codependent attitudes and behaviors people learn in dysfunctional families of origin affect the types of religious groups they later seek out.

Low Self-Esteem

A person's lack of self-worth, symptomatic of core shame created by childhood abuse, neglect or trauma, can easily be confused with humility and spiritual progress. This misperception is especially true for religious groups that see ego and individuality as barriers to spiritual growth. Most mystical systems are set up to transcend the ego, but that practice rests on the presumption that people who come to the group are relatively whole. Unless spiritual teachers understand how the self gets fragmented in childhood trauma, they may inadvertently reward beginners for codependency.

Anna told me of a scrape she had with a dysfunctional religious group. Having completed years of Jungian analysis, she felt a strong need to work again on spiritual development. Because of several negative experiences with the Holy Order of Mans, she was terrified of this longing. To gain clarity about how to overcome what was building to a crisis, a friend suggested that she spend some time at a center run by an enlightened teacher.

After a week-long retreat, the teacher managed to convince Anna that they had been lovers in a former lifetime and that it would benefit Anna's spiritual growth if she would sell her business, give him her house, and devote her life to working for the organization he wanted to build. For two weeks, she was excited by this prospect, then she began to pay attention to ways she had been manipulated. Heeding her gut reaction, she severed ties with the group.

Throughout the next month, I heard rave reviews from spiritual cynics who were convinced to hear this teacher speak. They were captivated by his magnetism and energy. Several people involved in the local organization had stopped eating, in imitation of the teacher's assistant, who was reportedly so spiritually advanced that she could exist on air alone. Because the leader used awkward hand and arm gestures when he spoke, his followers, too, began twitching when they talked. The number of female followers who had been his lovers in former lifetimes was truly astonishing. People stopped child support payments, because they were certain that all worldly ties are illusory. Their lack of ego strength and individuality were the very attributes which, they were taught, marked them as advanced beings.

The next time I saw Anna, she told me her thoughts about this new group. "How can you give up an ego if you don't have one yet?"

she questioned. "These people are the ones who are severely hurt by this process." With little sense of self, such people are usually adult children of dysfunctional families living out their codependence in a religious setting.

Lack of Balance

When inexperienced people or those with low self-esteem are drawn to the intense energy some spiritual groups and teachers emit, tragedy can result. Even though a teacher or a group may not deliberately set out to damage people, followers who lack a solid sense of self are easily tipped off balance. "Their worlds are dumped upside down," Anna says. "They want to quit their jobs and just go out and love people, with no consciousness about what they're doing. They still have to support themselves. These people are devastated."

Her awakening to the true nature of the group came, not only from her own interactions with the teacher, but from the experiences of others in the group. She explains, "A friend of mine, a younger woman, now says, `I want to cut those terrible things out of my soul. Why do they feel like they know something I don't? Am I supposed to quit everything and go live with them?' That's the kind of thing that happened to me before. It's emotionally unhealthy."

Even though going overboard is emotionally unhealthy, it is fairly typical for codependents to see things in all-or-nothing terms. They either totally reject people, ideas, and groups, or they completely embrace them to the exclusion of everything else. Their enthusiasm knows no bounds; if a little is good, more must surely be better. Extremists find it difficult to imagine a middle ground because, while growing up, they did not see that modeled. Unfortunately, when they go overboard, they are in deep trouble if they do not know how to swim— or if the water is shark infested.

Rigidity and Perfectionism

Rather than support our individual needs and growth, dysfunctional families force us to mold ourselves to their distorted shape. We learn to fit in at all costs, and the price of disagreeing or even asking questions is enormous. Setting impossibly high standards of perfection for ourselves, we channel all of our energy into looking good on the outside. It becomes second nature to cling to rigid thinking and perfectionism. We see the world in dichotomies: complete enlightenment or total ignorance, true faith or heresy, sin or righteousness, heaven or hell, salvation or damnation. As far as we are concerned, there are no gray areas in life, and little room for common sense.

The Florida Baptist college Susan attended was religious, but a far cry from the hellfire and brimstone she'd experienced as a teenager during summer camp in upstate New York. "I danced my shoes off," she says. "I was rebellious, but at that point I didn't care. Then in my junior year I got into Young Life, a conservative evangelical group. Since I was minoring in psychology, I started to work as a counselor with them. My motivation was guilt and fear. I was a little nervous with my rebelling and I needed to get back into strict belief."

After Susan earned a degree in art, her doubts began. College had helped her to see life from a perspective beyond the Plymouth Brethren brand of Christianity she had been raised in. To clarify her beliefs, she spent the next summer doing graduate work in Christian Studies at the Young Life Institute. Although the experience allowed for some questioning, her fellow classmates were very conservative in their beliefs, and she pushed herself to conform.

She was accepted at the Menninger Foundation, in Kansas, as an art therapist. During the three-year period she worked there, she met her husband, Bill, who had been raised a Baptist. "We didn't give a lot of thought to religion, except we both felt it was important to marry a conservative, evangelical Christian," she says.

After their first child was born and Bill graduated from law school, the couple moved to the Upper Midwest. The guilt and fear from Susan's childhood came flooding back as the couple thought about how to raise their baby. "You can put religious issues on hold, but they burst into full bloom when you have children," she says. "We struggled with it until it became an obsession."

As a result, Bill and Susan became involved in the charismatic renewal movement within the Episcopal church, a choice they believed would allow them conservatism within a liberal denomination. "In the Episcopal church you didn't hear a lot about sin and Satan, but there was still that fundamentalist element in the charismatic movement," says Susan. "We struggled intellectually and spiritually with the whole subject of our religion."

Over the next decade, Susan and Bill immersed themselves in charismatic renewal, culminating when they and two other families decided to form a Christian community in the countryside. Pooling all their funds, they purchased eighty-five acres and two houses. One of the families lived in the smaller house, while Susan, Bill, and their two young children shared the larger house with the other family.

"We were living and breathing it," says Susan. "More people came to our prayer meetings until about thirty-five were regulars. For five years we gave everything we had, trying to make the community work and the project took on a rigid, fundamentalist mind-set. Once you've done critical thinking, it is very difficult to push yourself into the fundamentalist mold, and we wound up having a tremendous conflict with the people we were living with. The more we tried and the deeper we went, the more it didn't work. We had to get that far out before we could wake up."

Denial of Our Own Perceptions and Feelings

Children growing up in dysfunctional families give more credence to what others tell us to think and feel than to what actually goes on inside ourselves. When we do attempt to think and act for ourselves, chances are we are punished. Over time, deferring to others becomes second nature. As a result, we sacrifice our needs and forget how to let our feelings guide us. Since we've schooled ourselves to ignore internal warning signals, we are tenaciously loyal, clinging to people and groups long after they have outlived their usefulness and have become spiritually stifling.

After years of denying feelings, we may not be able to recognize our internal emotional states. Renee, who eventually left the convent, reflects that some people find it easier than she did to leave a religious organization that ceased to promote growth. "I knew people in the seventh grade who went through confirmation, decided it was for the birds, and walked away in a healthy way," she comments. "Maybe they come into the world with more wisdom or on another path. Maybe they got enough self-confidence as children to trust themselves."

Renee's spiritual growth has involved becoming a massage therapist. She views this career change as an attempt to reconnect with her body and emotions, things she was completely cut off from during the first half of her life. "The body tells us what we need to know," she says. "It is a tool we're given by God, yet our families and most of our religions don't honor it. If our body suffers, we're told it's God's punishment. The body isn't something to rejoice in or to trust."

Communication and Intimacy Problems

Because life in a dysfunctional family cuts us off from knowing what we feel and need, we have difficulty sharing feelings and assertively telling others what we need. Instead, we guess what we're supposed to feel or want and then act the part. This inability to clearly know or communicate who we are means we have few skills for setting boundaries. Some of us find dysfunctional religious groups attractive because they "force" us to cut off our parents, something we have not had the courage to do ourselves.

With our lack of balance, we view intimacy from an either-or perspective. Either we build impenetrable barriers between ourselves and others, or we fuse with them. This boundary-erecting and boundary-blurring dynamic can play itself out within the groups we join when we give mixed messages to our teachers and fellow believers, telling them, in effect, to "go away closer." Even in relatively healthy spiritual settings, our lack of communication skills and difficulty with intimacy can cause relationships to sour.

As soon as Brenda joined the Sufi school, childhood issues of trust started surfacing. "My family was dysfunctional, and I had no friends as a child," she says. "I lived in a fantasy world. People probably regarded me as semiautistic at times." Her relationship with her spiritual teacher, she feels, wasn't an attempt to be reparented. Instead it was like being parented for the first time and she wasn't sure how to react. "My teacher was kind to me," she says. "He held me when I was crying, and that was the first time that had happened to me. I was used to being hit or ignored when I was crying."

In time, however, the early feelings of security ended. When her teacher told her she needed to stop approaching the world in an overly intellectual manner, she responded by secretly monitoring her speech patterns to avoid ever using three-syllable words, and for a year she gave up reading, a lifelong passion. After months of this self-imposed vigilance, she began to distrust her spiritual mentor and eventually viewed him as an enemy, much as she had viewed all adults as a child. Finally, she shut down completely but still attended group meetings.

Brenda's years away from the group have given her a much different perspective on what happened. Now she has come to the conclusion that she acted unfairly by expecting her mentor to read her mind. "I don't believe he knew how I was responding to his cues," she reports. "While I didn't use three-syllable words, he considered my statements emotional and didn't criticize them. He's from Kuwait and spoke very poor English, so probably some of his requests to me to modify my speaking were because he didn't understand me. I overreacted. I wish I had been able to tell him what was going on with me. Instead, I shut down and didn't communicate. Then I left the group."

Brenda says she wasn't emotionally strong enough to remain in the group. It took her four or five years of introspection to fully understand what she had learned about herself from this experience. "Some teachings were just a seed to me, and my life had to evolve before I could integrate them. My teacher didn't understand me psychologically, so although he tried to help me, he just didn't know how."

Compulsions and Addictions

With no thought to our own identity, our pattern of living through and for others can lead to total dependence on others to validate our existence and erase our shame. Since getting approval is the only way we feel good about ourselves, we may even violate our values to gain approval. Terrified of their anger and possible rejection, we narrow our focus until nothing else matters but the person or group to which we have become attached.

When we use religious teachers and groups to numb childhood pain, the more immersed we become in religiosity and the less effective we are in our daily lives. A downward spiral of problems and pain, followed by more spiritual striving, soon creates more problems and pain.

A year after Crystal caught her husband kissing another woman under the mistletoe, he divorced her to marry the other woman. Crystal reacted by involving herself even more deeply in church activities. A year later she met her second husband in the charismatic church. "I felt safe with him, because of where I'd met him," she confides, "but I didn't love him. The great wounds I had received in my childhood and my former marriage caused me to put up many walls. We were married for twenty-seven years."

Those years were busy ones. Crystal became an ordained minister and spent eighteen years doing missionary work, fifteen in Colombia. Partly to grow spiritually, Crystal and her new husband volunteered to be missionaries. Even though she felt she made some progress, she was still miserable. "I always felt inadequate, that I was flawed, that there was something wrong with my personality. I prayed about it many times and felt like I didn't know what to do about it," she says.

To cope with her shame, she turned even more fervently to her religion for solace. "For me religious addiction was an escape," she says. I couldn't be happy unless I was doing something for or with the church. I tried to get all my self-worth, all my self-esteem, from my religion."

Today she is convinced that the conservative religious organization was attractive to her because it appeared to be the opposite of what she had grown up with—a sadistic and sexually abusive father. Even in South America, the incest of her childhood continued to haunt her, despite her constant involvement with religious activities. "I felt unstable and insecure around men. I felt dirty," she explains. "I couldn't say anything about it in the church; they would look at me suspiciously."

Working hard on her recovery today, Crystal stresses that she doesn't blame the church for her obsessive behavior. "All of my problems were about me, my history, and the way I was raised to look at things." She also stresses that she wasn't alone in using religion as a pain reliever. "I think back to my years in the church and feel heartbroken because so many people are just escaping, using the church like drugs or alcohol, because they need to have some way to cope."

She continues: "Obviously I'd buried my childhood wounds, and until I can work through them, I will not be whole. Lots of churches won't have anything to do with psychology; they say it's bad. When you've been wounded in childhood, you can go to church and pray. That's important, but you have to do the gut work, too."

Religion Versus Psychology

When we are unaware of the psychological baggage we bring to our spiritual quest, we can be distracted from the serious psychological work we need to do. Some religious groups forbid therapy, even regarding it as evil. Other groups, while not condemning psychology outright, regard such help as unnecessary for people who are sincere in their beliefs. Seeking help from a therapist or a Twelve Step group is judged a sign of weakness and a lack of faith. Even though the group's teachings don't always discourage psychological work for adult children or childhood trauma victims, individual leaders may do so.

Ironically, the primary reason for an adult child to join such a group may stem from a need to heal from childhood trauma and abuse, or to discover why these were inflicted on us. If spiritual growth doesn't reduce our psychic pain, we perceive ourselves as failures and try to be more pious.

Spiritual development and emotional healing affect each other synergistically. People recovering from addictions and compulsions, as well as people resolving childhood issues in therapy, often use their psychological healing process as a springboard to spiritual exploration. Through membership in AA or other groups, they experience a spiritual awakening. Later they begin to seek a religious home beyond the self-help group because, despite their spiritual emphasis, these groups aren't designed to completely fulfill the function of a religion or spiritual practice.

Prayer and meditation may encourage previously suppressed childhood memories to surface. Ministers and spiritual teachers may not be knowledgeable enough to handle these memories constructively. Few are trained to handle posttraumatic stress disorder, multiple personality disorder, or the other very real legacies of childhood abuse. Our spiritual mentor might tell us to do something about a chemical addiction, but beyond informing us to stop using, he or she may offer few concrete techniques about how to maintain sobriety.

Even though psychology and spirituality aren't mutually exclusive, we make a major mistake when we fail to see and respect their very real differences. Psychology helps us deal with our emotions and live more effectively. Spirituality helps us transcend the material world for an awareness of union with the Divine. The two disciplines work on different levels. Expecting one to do the job of the other is like consulting a psychologist instead of an orthopedist for a broken leg.

At certain times and in certain areas of our lives, a focus on discipline, obedience, and authority may be appropriate. At other times and in other areas, we need to develop a clearer sense of ourselves as individuals. Anna comments, "Some spiritual groups say psychological therapy is intellectual, leading you around in a circle and never helping you get anywhere. Psychology may do that,but there are approaches that move people forward."

While some dysfunctional religious groups ignore psychology, others may use their own brand of counseling as a lure to attract new members. Typically, such groups forbid members to enter into a relationship with a trained therapist. Scientology is one such group. Before the auditing process developed by founder L. Ron Hubbard, new recruits undergo a "life repair." "You review your life and take a look at the trouble you've had," says Tracy. "You talk about it with your auditor, much as you would in standard psychotherapy."

The auditing process is designed to detect and clear away points of pain in the unconsciousness of which people are unaware in the wakeful state. Tracy explains, "It's like regression. You go back and find significant moments in this life or another life and bring them up to the conscious level so that they don't have power in your life. The technique works; healing does occur. But then that healing is put to the service of power and wealth for the organization."

Tracy says that, in Scientology, both psychology and psychiatry are considered evils. Members who receive therapy at any point are forever forbidden access to higher-level teaching materials. "These teachings focus mainly on mystical abilities to create in your life what you choose to create, while avoiding the problems most human beings encounter. Denying access to traditional therapy is a way to control people. It also screens out people who wouldn't totally buy into the system, people who would question."

CHAPTER SIX

Conversion or Coercion? Understanding Religious Manipulation

Even though leaders of dysfunctional religious groups may vilify psychology, they are masters of psychological persuasion. They skillfully use high-pressure techniques to swell the group's ranks and enrich bank accounts. Far from being esoteric or alien, these potent spiritual sales strategies are similar to ones encountered daily, from advertisers selling a new shade of eye shadow or the latest model car. Not only do such leaders have inherent power to persuade, but most people do not expect to encounter such manipulation in a spiritual context. Believing that religion is synonymous with good intentions, even the brightest and best educated are willing to entrust psyche and soul to a fast-talking stranger.

The spectre of a sinister cult recruiter snatching people off the streets into spiritual bondage is terrifying but is most often fantasy. People who talked with me did not feel they had been recruited against their wills or brainwashed initially by the groups. Rather, group recruiters are experts at reading and appearing to meet deep-seated needs. Hence, they have little trouble appealing to potential members who were looking for something to believe in and seemed to find a caring, trustworthy group. Although initial involvement was a matter of choice, once involved, new recruits were often subjected to potent persuasion campaigns designed to mold their attitudes, beliefs, and actions to fit the group's desires. Leaving the organization soon became excruciatingly difficult.

After her stint at a yoga ashram in California, Tracy returned to her college town and moved into a house with several other young people. She was 21. When a housemate attended a Scientology lecture and urged everyone else to go, Tracy went along. At the meeting she saw material on past lives. Finally, it seemed as though she might be able to find some answers to questions raised by her earlier experiences.

By this time she had given up school to devote herself completely to her search for understanding. "I had decided nothing was more important than finding out who God is, who I am, and if I had lived before," she says. Motivated to become a Scientologist, she moved to Los Angeles to be closer to the main organization.

Remembering her seven-year involvement with Scientology, she now says, "Groups like this are effective at getting members because they hook you with truth. People recognize truth, and one of the great truths Scientology teaches is that you are not just a body, you are a spirit with a body. When I joined, that was a radical thought in white suburban America.

She did not know that the inner workings of the organization were diametrically opposed to what was being taught, until she became a part of the group's leadership circle.

Stated beliefs and teachings may promote growth, but a group's hidden agendas and dynamics can destroy. Although the people who shared their stories didn't believe they had been forced to become members, like Tracy, several believed they had initially been lied to and finally betrayed.

Unfriendly Persuasion

In a pluralistic society where religious freedom is protected, no truth-in-advertising laws exist to protect the innocent and overly trusting from religious con artists. We must exercise caution, but responding to the slightest hint of persuasion with total skepticism isn't effective either. If we turned our backs on every spiritual group that tried to share its beliefs with us, we would eliminate the vast majority of organized religions from our lives.

Religious people who believe they know truth and have a system for salvation or enlightenment want to tell other people about it. Sharing the good news, or evangelizing, may be seen as a moral duty. In recent years, membership drives shaped by marketing strategies, including demographic studies, advertising campaigns, and follow-up contacts have been used to reach people who are unchurched. Although the individuals who try to convert others may become overzealous, most are sincerely concerned and do not deliberately misrepresent their faith.

It is natural for a group to try to make a good first impression. Whether the church across town invites you to an ice cream social or the temple down the street requests your presence for High Holidays, chances are you'll be made to feel welcome. You're unlikely to hear about the power struggle on the board of trustees or the abortion conflict that is causing a bitter split in the congregation. Members will smile at you, shake your hand firmly, engage you in small talk, and urge you to come back. Once you decide you do not want to be a member, you can leave without pressure. If you try to leave a dysfunctional religious group, however, you will be covertly or blatantly manipulated into staying.

Smiles, handshakes, and small talk are techniques used by dysfunctional groups, too, as they attempt to win people over. Instead of assisting seekers to form a closer relationship with a Higher Power, in many cases they use membership to build the group's power or financial base. To bolster the organization, fund-raising may supplant teaching or even worship. Group members are sometimes expected to convert others to raise their own status within the group or to secure themselves a position in the afterlife. As soon as religious groups set recruitment quotas and focus on dollar signs rather than on enhancing relationships with the Divine, ethics suffer. To boost the body count or bank account, recruiters may disguise the group's identity or lie about the organization's teachings or true purposes.

Scientologists pose as small-business financial experts, luring dentists and chiropractors to take workshops designed to convert them. Other groups use stress-reduction seminars as a covert recruiting tool. A group calling itself The Brooklyn Greens, after the legitimate European Green political movement, has posed as environmentalists to recruit members and funnel them into the parent organization. The movement's stated goal is to break down all belief systems operating in the world today. The more dysfunctional the group, the greater the chances that this bait-and-switch tactic will be rationalized away as a means to a sacred end.

The Mystical Manipulation Process

In addition to fraudulent advertising, severely dysfunctional religious groups also resort to psychological manipulation and social control to teach and maintain expected behaviors and accepted beliefs. After joining the group, a new member becomes the target of an intensive and often unethical effort aimed at weaning them from the life they knew and bonding them permanently to the group. Although this manipulation isn't brainwashing in the classical sense, it can be difficult to resist.

Bob's parents made him attend Sunday School as a child, and as an adolescent he went to church on holidays only to make them happy. At 23, he set out to find his own church. Before starting his search, he spoke to a woman at work. "I started talking to her as she was going over some notes from a religious retreat," he says. "I really wanted to learn more about the Bible, and she told me about her church, the Denver Church of Christ. She said they had fun with God." That intrigued Bob. This sect, affiliated with the Boston Church of Christ and not a part of the more familiar Protestant denomination, believes that women are inferior and cannot teach men, so she referred Bob to the group's campus ministry.

"In early October I went to Bible talks that I assumed were Bible studies, but they really weren't," he says of his initial involvement. "They'd read a passage and talk about it in a very light vein. Only after a while did I find that the purpose wasn't study, but recruitment. You'd bring somebody you know. Then you'd take the talk leader aside so he could focus the Bible talk on a passage that had to do with the newcomer. Afterwards the recruiter would say to the person, 'Amazing, this just happened to do with you!'"

Open-minded and eager to learn, Bob trusted the group members and formed friendships. "I didn't have an inkling that they were trying to manipulate me, so I wasn't trying to be careful," he says. "I assumed cults were from the Far East; I didn't think they were Christian based. Of course, back then I didn't know that Reverend Moon used to be a

Presbyterian minister." A recent transplant to Denver from Montana, Bob had no social life and was excited to make new friends.

From the beginning he was assigned a discipler who was in charge of bringing him into the fold. The discipler quickly became his best friend, and his conversion proceeded so rapidly that it still remains a blur in Bob's mind today. After the Bible talks came a series of eight one-on-one Bible studies with the discipler. "One week I started the Bible studies, thinking they'd be once a week, and the next week I wanted to get in two a day, just so I could be baptized sooner. Baptism is a big lure," he explains.

Even though he had been baptized as a child in the Presbyterian church, he was required to repeat the sacrament again in the manner that the Boston Church of Christ prescribed. "I was immersed in ice water, which should have shaken me out of it, but it didn't," he says. "To go from agnostic to evangelical in a month is a huge change. I had been introverted and was trying to be an extrovert. I was a physics student and thought about dropping out of school to become a missionary. Before I had assumed I could use what I had gained in school to help whatever church I chose. The only thing the Boston Church of Christ has a use for is missionaries in order to win more converts."

By the end of that month, Bob was spending about forty hours a week at group members' houses, beginning as soon as he left school or work. In addition to Sunday activities, gatherings were held every night of the week except Wednesdays, which were reserved for the one-on-one meetings with disciplers. "It was exhausting," he comments. "We'd stay up until two or three o'clock in the morning, then everybody would be up again at six or seven. I didn't have time to think."

The decrease in Bob's critical thinking ability and the growth of his total loyalty to his new church was exactly what the group wanted to ensure. Far from being exotic or illegal, the persuasion tactics used on Bob seemed so ordinary he didn't regard them as manipulation at all. Because he was exhausted by the schedule and unaware of what was happening, these strategies were extremely effective and Bob left the group only after outside intervention.

Strategies for Social Control

Dysfunctional religious groups apply their persuasive strategies in an individual manner. In some groups the intensification phase—the early high-pressure persuasion phase—may not arrive until members move up the hierarchy. Those more loosely affiliated with the group are able to come and go as they please. Tracy says, "I wasn't coerced when I joined Scientology. The mind control didn't happen until I joined the staff and became part of the inner circle." Other groups, like the Boston Church of Christ, may be manipulative from the first contact.

Being vulnerable to this pressure doesn't indicate mental inadequacy or emotional disturbance. We tend to react automatically in certain situations. These predictable reactions may have actually fostered the survival of the human species and may be biologically based. When we encounter a skillful manipulator who knows exactly how to reach us, it's hard not to be swayed. None of these techniques is inherently destructive; it is the purpose for which they are used that makes them destructive. Even though we're told we can walk away from a group at any time, unless we're consciously aware of being manipulated, we can be overwhelmed with a sense of paralyzing inertia, unable to disentangle ourselves but not understanding why we feel so stuck.

Love Bombing

Few people can resist unconditional love. Even those who grew up with plenty of love hunger for more, especially when lonely or going through a transition. When we meet people who appear to love us without strings attached, we're flattered. If they compliment us and hug us and hang on every word we say, we're even more flattered. We're so pleased to be basking in all this attention and instant rapport, we may never stop to ask ourselves whether it's selfless and sincere. In many cases it isn't, and we may have granted trust to someone supremely unworthy of that trust.

Reciprocation

People with hidden agendas often give gifts—flowers and books, meals and parties, retreats and concerts. When we receive things we haven't asked for, we feel obligated to reciprocate. Our uneasiness leads to an effort to repay our imaginary debt as quietly as possible.

Unaware of what we're doing, we may inadvertently make a long-term commitment to a group based on a desire to reciprocate for a gift of a dozen carnations.

Emotional Release

Swept away by instant intimacy and group camaraderie, people find it easy to let go emotionally. After provoking a man to cry, members comfort him. They listen as a woman shares her deepest secrets. Those who refuse to drop their defenses are told that reluctance to be emotionally vulnerable is jeopardizing their spiritual progress and that they are too intellectual. True religious experiences are seldom purely intellectual; on the other hand, being completely defenseless with strangers leaves people emotionally off balance and at the mercy of others.

Fear and Paranoia

Vulnerable people are especially susceptible to scare tactics. Group leaders may attempt to convince people that theirs is the only way to salvation, and that those who do not follow their teachings are doomed. Suspicion of outsiders who don't share the group's belief system is encouraged. Often, vague and shadowy terrors are used to keep followers in line.

Regression to Childhood

Some spiritual leaders encourage regression to childhood by treating members like children. They frighten them into obedience with stories about spiritual boogeymen. Subjected to hours of singing simple songs and playing childhood games, members feel small. Regression puts new recruits in a docile and dependent frame of mind and creates the illusion of a loving religious family. Often members view the group's leader as a parent.

Authority

Once we begin to view a spiritual leader as an authority, we are more inclined to accept this person's views without question. Sometimes we obey this person's authority even though doing so violates our own values. As evidenced by the famous Milgrim studies discussed later in this book, people are willing to administer shocks they believe are incredibly painful to the victim with no more coercion than having a white-coated "scientist" tell them to. While our tendency to follow the leader—whether a supervisor, a politician, or a professor—works in our favor much of the time, in some circumstances it is extremely dangerous.

Disorientation and Confusion

Many dysfunctional religious groups disorient and confuse new members by overwhelming them with a barrage of complex experiences and teachings on top of little sleep and fasting. Unsure of themselves, the new members desperately try to regain a sense of balance and may accept the first answer given to their questions.

Altered States

When we expect to be deeply moved, we usually are. Dysfunctional religious groups often interpret our profound internal experiences in ways that enable such experiences to serve the group's purposes. Although not damaging in their own right, religious rituals that produce altered states of consciousness can leave people vulnerable to suggestion. Such states are relatively easy to produce. After meditation, chanting, or prolonged singing of hymns, information is incorporated at a deeper level of consciousness than when simply listening to a lecture. For many centuries, altered states have been used to trigger mystical experiences.

Isolation

One of the most disorienting techniques a group can use is isolation. Sometimes silence and isolation are practiced in weekend or week-long camps. Because members have severed ties with families and friends there is little chance to compare what is being taught with anything outside the group. The only worldview, then, is the one the group approves. Under these circumstances, members may come to depend completely on the dysfunctional group to provide validation. Many healthy groups offer weekend retreats, too, but isolation or silence is never forced, and retreat goers can break silence or isolation any time they choose.

Information Control

Once inside a dysfunctional religious group, we have only limited access to information that contradicts the organization's position. Even though we may not be in an isolated commune, we may be discouraged from reading, listening to news programs, or attending functions given by other religious groups. We're told that these things will confuse us and lead us off the true path. This information control has the effect of insulating us in a cocoonlike frame of reference. It's often so warm and snug inside that cocoon, we're lulled into staying. We stop questioning, because without input from the world outside our group, we find it difficult to even formulate questions.

Peer Pressure

What other people think of us can influence our decision-making processes, as well. If everyone else in the group seems to accept the leader's directions without question, we may go along simply to fit in or to avoid making waves. By conforming, we avoid drawing undue attention to ourselves and ensure that people in the group will continue to give us the unconditional positive regard we've come to know and love. At the beginning of our involvement, we may act as if we believe something we really don't in order to gain acceptance. Eventually we internalize the acted beliefs. After all, cooperation is a virtue—one most of us have been taught since childhood.

Exclusivity

The temptation of being part of a group that has a cosmic secret is tantalizing. When our group's teachings are packaged as being accessible only to the chosen, we can't help but be a little smug. We are spiritually superior to most other human beings simply because we joined the group. Because we think a group's teachings or time with the leader is a rare and precious commodity, we will place a higher value on them and work harder to get them.

Commitment

Often dysfunctional religious groups push a member to make a public commitment to them before the member is ready. Once we've openly stated our affiliation with the group, whether by walking to the altar to be saved, allowing our phone number to be printed on a brochure, or signing a contract, few of us are willing to go back on our word. We have a strong interest in keeping any kind of pledge we've made. Changing our minds seems an admission of being weak willed, at best, or a liar.

Self-renunciation

Often dysfunctional religious groups demand more than our promise of loyalty. They want our time, our earthly possessions, and our talents. If we are serious, they tell us, we'll give up what is most important to us as a form of service and a symbolic gesture to prove that we are no longer slaves to our egos and possessions. Once we've invested our time and money in a group, we'll do almost anything to keep reassuring ourselves that we've made the right decision. This may take the form of self-blaming and trying harder when the group wants us to do things that go against our ethics. If we're asked to give up our God-given talents, whether in art or engineering, to lick envelopes or stand on street corners selling candy and winning converts, we may even see that as punishment for past sins. Our relinquishment diminishes our self-esteem and makes us easier to manipulate.

Although we may be fully functional before being beseiged with these tactics, within a period of days we can be dramatically changed. Once a member is securely enmeshed within the group structure, he or she may be convinced that emotional or even physical survival is impossible outside the group. The more we incorporate the group's view, the more fearful we become that we'll be unable to function without it. To cut ourselves off from the group becomes, in our minds, the same as cutting ourselves off from God.

Steven Hassan, exit counselor and former Moonie, has experienced mind control and copes with this trauma by forming another identity distinct from the real self. Hassan's description of this mechanism in his book *Combating Cult Mind Control* is similar to the process by which childhood victims of incest and physical abuse split off fragmented personalities to absent themselves from the horrors they cannot escape. Psychologists and researchers have begun diagnosing post-traumatic stress disorder in people who have left such groups and have termed recent cult survivors "the walking wounded."

The Codependency Factor

Tracy and Bob were raised in healthy families that supported their needs and fostered their self-esteem, yet each succumbed to religious manipulation and within their dysfunctional groups behaved in codependent ways. Recovery from involvement with a dangerously manipulative spiritual group is often a long and difficult process even for people who start out with a solid sense of self. For people who were abused as children or who grew up in dysfunctional families, the effects of an intense persuasion campaign by a religious group that mirrors old family dynamics may be especially potent. We don't have to be taught to be codependent; we already know the rules to that game by heart. If we grew up in a home where denial was the rule, we may not recognize deception or doublespeak because we've come to accept that from authority figures. When rewarded for low self-esteem, living through others, and compliance, we may feel right at home. Our problem behaviors have miraculously been transformed into spiritual virtues—or so we're told.

People from dysfunctional or abusive backgrounds may not be more gullible than others but may have more to gain from these groups: identity, reparenting, and a chance to focus on the needs of others to the exclusion of self. Throughout college, Al excelled because he did everything that was expected of him and he worked hard to fit into the social structure. He met his wife, Rhonda, during a period of agnosticism, and although he had rejected the teachings of the Catholic Church, he still struggled to please his parents. Rhonda became pregnant as a consequence of Al's lingering uneasiness about using birth control, and they married.

The couple had other children and paid little attention to religion until Rhonda discovered that a spiritual group that provided opportunities to make friends and broaden her social horizons. Even though they found its rules too rigid, for a year they settled into the Baha'i Faith. Shortly after they pulled away from this variation of Islam, Rhonda's brother, Steve, became immersed in The Way International, a fundamentalist Christian sect. Steve wrote long and zealous letters that the couple joked about. Explains Al, "These letters went on and on about how great the leader was. Al raved so much, we really felt he'd been brainwashed."

Rhonda left Al with their four children to attend her brother's wedding at The Way headquarters in Ohio. When she returned, she was a born-again Christian. "She didn't think The Way was as much a religion as it was people who loved each other unconditionally," he says. "She wanted more of it, so she drove over one hundred miles to fellowship with Christians with similar views. It's interesting how *religion* is a bad word in The Way. They profess to be irreligious or even antireligious, but in reality they are a religion."

Al's reaction was a mixture of anger and despair. "These Christians fit my expectations perfectly," he says. "They eagerly anticipated the end of the world. They smoked like chimneys. They didn't believe in environmentalism. At first I thought it was the end of my marriage, and we had preschool kids. I'd never be able to go along with this Way stuff. My wife and three kids were about to be torn away from me by this steamroller called Christianity."

Soon, though, Al's old pattern of compliance returned, and to please Rhonda, he began attending fellowships. One meeting marked a turning point for him. At this gathering, Way members showed a music video from the album called "America Awakes," which the group had produced. While the moderator talked, Al noticed that the video tape deck was on. "I thought it was a waste of energy, so I turned it off, not realizing the tape had been cued up and I had screwed it up. I'd cut off the power to drive the message into people's brains. From the beginning I was suspect." Even though he wasn't called the anti-Christ, Al immediately felt judged as a heretic and a threat.

At a subsequent meeting, reference was made to the unforgivable sin of being born again in the devil. Afraid that this might be the reason he couldn't bring himself to convert, Al asked to know more about it and was handed a Way textbook. He was then told to sit alone in a room and read it. As he read, he learned that The Way taught that until rebirth in Christ, human beings are no more valuable than animals. To be born again in the devil is to be cast even lower. Unfortunately, people who are born of the devil appear altruistic and are the last people to be aware of their plight. "When I came out I didn't say anything," says Al. "I put the knowledge inside and wondered about it for twelve years."

He tried to conform by taking classes in The Way's theology but often found himself playing out a role that belied what was actually going on inside of him. "At the culmination of the foundational class everybody stands up and speaks in tongues," Al explains. "Prior to that the group leader says, 'Nobody has ever failed to speak in tongues in my class.' It's ultimate pressure. You stand up, close your eyes, breathe, try to relax, and then you speak in tongues. If you don't really know whether you're speaking in tongues or not, you fake it because you're afraid to be a freak."

Since he could see no way of arguing Rhonda out of her religious views, Al subjected himself to a thirty-eight-hour marathon of teaching tapes. "At four o'clock one morning, I made a decision to believe the Bible," he reports. His commitment lasted most of his adult life.

The Feel-Good Feeling

Even the most dysfunctional religious groups may give members extremely positive experiences at the start. Researcher Marc Galanter believes these organizations provide a biologically based relief effect to new recruits. Initially, then, we feel much better about ourselves, and our problems seem to be resolved. It's the same sort of immediate relief that self-help groups give desperate sufferers.

New to San Francisco, flat broke, and burning out on drugs at 19, John accepted the dinner invitation offered by a friendly woman on Polk Street. After finishing his food, he heard a lecture on the Divine Principal, the teachings of Reverend Moon. "I had a conversion experience that night," he says. "I felt the teaching was true and I wanted to explore it." The next day he left for a northern California farm owned by the Unification Church. "For two years afterward I didn't smoke, I didn't drink, and I didn't have sex," he says. "Those compulsions were lifted, and I didn't go through withdrawal." John lived at the farm for a few months and spent his time tending the garden and listening to lectures. Later he was sent to Florida to work as a sales representative for the group's health food line. Eventually he ended up in New York City doing advertising for a Unification Church–owned company. Although his abstinence lasted only as long as his ties to the church, it was a very positive change in his life, one he remains grateful for.

Brenda, too, believes her involvement with groups, even the neurotic ones, contributed to her growth on some level. "If I went into a so-called cult and came out with 75 percent of my problems, that meant a quarter of them had been resolved," she says. "I look at that as progress."

Brenda was looking for psychological healing, not spirituality, when she attended workshops offered by the Sufi-based school, so she was highly skeptical at the start. Her attachment to her teacher impelled her to continue attending meetings. "My behavior could be described as Freudian transference. I would have done anything he wanted," she says. "Because my teacher thought it was a good idea for people to join his group, I joined. I didn't go in with a spiritual focus. I learned a spiritual focus that I would not have had otherwise."

While neither John nor Brenda advocates deliberately joining a dysfunctional religious group, they serve as examples that not everything that happens in such groups is negative. Life in these organizations is often a combination of positive, uplifting experiences and damaging manipulation. That mixture is a potent brew that can further our enmeshment in much the same way that love-hate relationships of childhood can keep one emotionally tied to a dysfunctional family long after reaching adulthood and moving away.

CHAPTER SEVEN

Déjà Vu—Dysfunctional Religious Family Dynamics

Dysfunctional religious groups exhibit interaction patterns similar to those seen in sexually, emotionally, or physically abusive families or in families with a chemically dependent member. Blurred boundaries, rigid hierarchies, and inflexible rules ensure the organization's survival at the expense of individual members' emotional needs and well-being.

The group's rules, whether or not they are spoken, may contradict philosophical stance or religious teachings. Even though spiritual development and loving behavior are stated goals, the organization's day-to-day dynamics may promote things other than growth and loving relationships. Like members of a dysfunctional family, group members often deny this paradox as they adapt to the group's codependent lifestyle. In both shame-based families and shame-based religious organizations, victims learn to live outside themselves, to ignore their perceptions of reality, suppress doubts, keep secrets, and try to appear perfect at all costs.

Emotional and physical distance between the group and outsiders creates a closed system, while boundaries between members weaken or disappear. Becoming enmeshed in a virtual armed fortress, believers fuse into an undifferentiated ego mass, trading autonomy and integrity for a sense of belonging as barriers between insiders and the outside world give the illusion of security. Group members then are extremely vulnerable to those higher in the power structure who dictate what to think and feel and how to act. Sometimes this enmeshment and boundary blurring extends to coerced sex.

The same dynamics that stifle one's growth in a troubled family keep one tightly bound to any unhealthy system. Breaking or questioning rules could lead to being shamed, ignored, or cut off from the people we relied on to meet our physical and emotional needs.

Similar consequences for rule-breaking hold sway in a religious group gone wrong. Since codependency is required for the group's survival, it is fostered and rewarded. Those who play by the rules advance within the hierarchy of the group and are deemed more spiritually advanced. Those who ask questions or refuse to obey face being shamed, shunned, or expelled. Since members have ceased to function as individuals and their identity is determined entirely by the group, being cast out can be a terrifying prospect.

Dysfunctional family dynamics abound at school, at work, and in social organizations. Some teachers run authoritarian classrooms, bosses may be emotionally abusive and dictatorial, and social clubs may turn into exclusionary hotbeds of unhealthy interactions. Though these encounters can drain people's energy and leave them emotionally bruised, they don't carry the same potential for damage as do similar interactions in families or the spiritual arena. Just as we depended on our families of origin to feed, clothe, and shelter us, we may depend on the dysfunctional religious group to meet our basic survival needs, especially if we've left our jobs and given them all our money. Even when we retain an independent living arrangement, if the religious group becomes the primary focus of our lives, we may be just as dependent on them for emotional nurturing as we once were on our families of origin. This neediness is underscored by our subconscious urge to be reparented by a religious authority figure.

Finally, since most unhealthy groups teach that their particular system is the sole path to enlightenment or the only way to the Divine, outcasts often feel that their connection to God has been severed. Once we've internalized an exclusionary belief system, most of us would do almost anything rather than confront the existential terror and shame of being dismissed from the earthly paradise we once believed in.

Once we give away our power, the group can dictate our spiritual, psychological, and physical fate.

Necessary Evils

Not all dysfunctional religious groups arise from a power-hungry charismatic leader out to gather a flock of loyal followers in order to fleece them. Most religious organizations begin with the best intentions. A person who believes he or she possesses a unique truth or method naturally wants to share it. Students assemble, and a group forms. What starts as an individual spiritual quest quickly becomes codified and structured into a new religion or sect, regardless of whether the leader initially planned it that way.

Groups cannot exist without boundaries that define them or an internal structure to direct their functions. Evidence shows that human beings are biologically impelled to join groups, not only to gain a sense of community, but to receive direction. Being told what to do frees us from some of the ambiguities, doubts, and frustrations characteristic of anyone's spiritual journey. Because of their boundaries and hierarchies, religious groups offer a safe haven from existential angst.

Healthy organizations—whether families, businesses, clubs, or religious groups—recognize that boundaries and power structures may be double-edged swords. Even as structures provide cohesion and enable the group to carry out tasks collectively, they can smother or imprison individuals in the group. Ideally an organization strives to maintain a balance between group needs and individual needs.

If individuals' needs are always the top priority, the group may cease to exist. On the other hand, if group needs always supersede those of the individual, the result is a totalitarian group. As old members are used up because their energy and ability to function have been sacrificed for the organization, new people are recruited to replace them. No member is indispensable. It is important to work toward achieving a delicate balance between meeting group and individual needs over time. Otherwise what was community building may become destructive either for the group as a whole or for its members.

A new religious group is often a closed system with an authoritarian or semiauthoritarian structure. Whether they've broken off from an established religion, grown up around a radically new set of teachings, or formed around old teachings transplanted from a different culture, new religious groups aren't part of the cultural mainstream. Society views them as deviant because their practices and teachings are different and may seem bizarre.

Group interactions with mainstream society may then automatically feel limited and hostile. At least initially, thick boundaries and feelings of persecution prevail. Early Christians who faced the ever-present possibility of martyrdom, and Eastern European Jews who lived with the threat of pogroms centuries later, weren't being paranoid when they formed tightly knit communities.

In addition to serving as protection, separation from society during initial formation ensures emotional bonding between members, a requirement if the group is to thrive. Before an organization can attract followers, there must be a clearly defined "something" to belong to. New groups may identify themselves as much by who they are as well as who they are not.

During a group's early formation, a strong, hierarchical system is necessary to help members form a unit to get the group's work done. All religious groups, even those solidly established as part of the dominant culture, occasionally must engage in recruitment and fund-raising. These tasks can be especially difficult for new organizations and doubly difficult for groups unfamiliar to the culture. Therefore, members' time and energy is channeled by strong leadership to recruit and raise funds so the group can survive and grow into an established institution.

Most well-established religions evidence some history of authoritarian rule. Moses was not the elected leader of the Jewish people; he was the patriarch appointed by God. In addition to being a religious ritual, circumcision not only reminded Jews of their covenant with God, but served to mark them as different from their Gentile neighbors. Christ appointed Peter as head of the church. Mohammed, too, had a mandate from Allah and a close circle of disciples who surrounded him.

While many established religious structures left their guerrilla tactics and cadrelike structures over time, vestiges of separateness and tight discipline remain. Even today some members of different faiths are advised to stick to their own kind. Although it may be permissible to work and socialize with nonbelievers, interfaith marriages are discouraged. Some religious leaders are regarded as possessing the ultimate truth. Even so, in most established religions at least some attempt is made to honor individual needs and contributions.

In a dysfunctional group, rigid rules and hierarchies aren't transitory features modified or discarded after group identity is established. Instead they become a permanent part of the organization's operation leading to excessive isolation and abusive autocratic leadership.

An Isolated Life

Whether members of a dysfunctional religious group live communally or separately, they are often urged to cut ties with those who don't belong to the organization. Dysfunctional religious groups label outsiders nonspiritual, or unenlightened, and prohibit "true believers" from contact with outsiders.

As members become more tightly enmeshed, they avoid former friends and family as contempt for nonbelievers is used to increase their loyalty to the group. The more isolated members become, the more they define themselves by the organization's identity. Even without directly being told, they believe that since all outsiders are flawed, they themselves will have no value if they leave the organization. The same fear, spawned by polarization, keeps members of dysfunctional families chained to their damaging systems.

Anna, who kept her apartment during her seven years with the Holy Order of Mans, found her time so filled with religious activities that she missed many days of work. "Every waking moment, I was occupied," she says. "There was morning Mass at 5:30 and then Bible study, group meetings, or something else every night of the week. For seven years the community became my whole world. I completely dropped out of my former life."

Extreme time commitments are common in dysfunctional religious groups because they increase members' reliance on the group to meet all psychological and spiritual needs. Anna's isolation and denial of her own individuality were encouraged by the group. Instead of being helped to discover and use her own internal resources, she was conditioned to rely solely on the group.

The effect of subordinating her needs to those of the Order for seven years left Anna devastated. Despite her efforts to fit in, many group members disliked her because of her relationship with her teacher. Their disapproval, instead of inspiring her to leave, spurred her to try harder to be one of the gang. When the group finally disbanded, Anna, in a last ditch effort to be accepted, threw a farewell party for her teacher. Afterward she sat in her empty apartment, lost. "I was forced back into the real world," she says. "I remember looking around and asking, 'What do I do now?' I didn't have a clue. I had divorced myself from my family, friends, everyone, because I was told this was the only way I would make it. My very salvation depended on my total commitment to the Holy Order."

Enemy Making

Beyond providing a cocoon that keeps members from experiencing the world, some groups raise even higher barriers by labeling outsiders as evil-minded enemies. Such extreme polarization encourages group members to circle their wagons against potential attacks from people so labeled. Although these feared attacks are sometimes real, reports have shown group leaders deliberately provoke conflicts with outsiders. By focusing on defending the group against supposed opposition, the members' attention is diverted from problems within the group. Just as a dysfunctional family might view a teacher or a social worker who could uncover family secrets as a hostile foe, some dysfunctional religious groups make newspaper reporters, the government, or psychiatrists the enemy.

Another danger outsiders pose is that they may lead believers from the intended path and the true faith. When convenient enemies don't materialize in the outside world, group leaders sometimes draw on the frightening possibility of supernatural evil powers to whip up paranoia. A punitive God who will deal harshly with those who question the faith is often used as a threat.

Although she is no longer a part of the fundamentalist sect in which she served as a missionary, Crystal still grapples with feelings of condemnation. "Because of my upbringing, I already have some problems with feeling condemned and judged," she says. "The church organization uses doctrines and Bible teachings to keep people from reading or listening to different things. The leader's Bible thumping and tone of voice are frightening. I believe in the wrath of God, but the Bible teaches gentleness and forgiveness. Bible beaters say they have all the answers. The more I search and reach for God, the less I know. I do know you find Him everywhere."

Whether members learn within the group's fear-provoking milieu that real enemies are out to get them or that the devil is after their souls, they are schooled that their separateness and isolation from the world provide protection. Terror at the thought of leaving the group or having contact with nonbelievers also inspires gratitude that the group exists. Confusion results since the rigidity that provokes discomfort also relieves it.

A similar double bind exists in dysfunctional families. To protect the secret of an alcoholic or abusive parent, children are forbidden to talk to nonfamily members and may be discouraged from playing with children other than their siblings. A sense of separateness is fostered so that children grow up to believe that any interaction with outsiders might invite ridicule or attack. They become grateful that the family unit protects them from judgment and rejection.

Groupthink

In dysfunctional religious groups, as in unhealthy families, information is filtered through the organization's censors. In some cases, members may be told that anything not overtly approved by the religious group is satanic. This also keeps members isolated in fear and makes any outside contact, even in the form of magazines or TV news programs, seem dangerous. Any action that might allow viewpoints other than those held by the organization is regarded as sinful, and to step across the group's clearly demarcated boundaries is grounds for condemnation and punishment. The resulting "groupthink" is accepted without question because members have few, if any, opportunities to compare what goes on within the group with life outside. Reality checking is limited to memories of the past, which dim as time passes or which members may be told are not reality.

Unique styles of worship, ritual, prayer, meditation, and other shared religious activities bind members into a more cohesive unit and are repeated until group culture replaces autonomous thinking. Dress, diet, living arrangements, and language also reinforce the barriers and promote unity and loyalty. For example, Tracy reports that Scientology has its own terms for many common words. The people working on

L. Ron Hubbard's ship were called the "Sea Org," sins were "overts." In time, people's goals and priorities change, recreation becomes centered on the group, and all facets of life come to serve as symbols of a new group-defined identity.

Demanding undivided allegiance, appropriating resources, suppressing independent decision making, and becoming members' sole emotional support, the dysfunctional religious group is transformed into a substitute family. It provides security in the form of acceptance and belonging. Reinforced loyalty and fusion with others powerfully cripples independent thought and action. With no frame of reference besides the organization, group members begin to lose their identity and readily accept harsh rules and authoritarian control.

Ritualized Relationships

Rules that separate members from outsiders must be repeatedly reinforced. Members must be watched closely for signs of deviation from group expectations. Once the group has grown, this task can no longer be accomplished by the leader and is often viewed as beneath his or her dignity. Deputies or apostles are handpicked to serve as religious middle managers.

In addition to making a group more efficient at accomplishing its goals, rigid and ritualized power structures reduce the risk that members will act spontaneously or think critically. Since discussion and shared decision making are believed to threaten the group's existence, dysfunctional religious groups avoid these at all costs.

The same power structure intent on patrolling the group's boundaries, delegating work, and providing punishment also enforces obedience and devotion. Members are told if they try harder, are faithful, patient, and conforming enough, perhaps they, like the chosen apostle or deputy, will someday be honored with a position of control over others.

Once he became a member of the Boston Church of Christ, Bob discovered a clearly delineated chain of command that left little room for dissent or discussion. "The Bible talks about being a disciple, and in most churches you're a disciple of Christ," he explains. "In the BCC, you're a disciple of your discipler because he's older in Christ, even if it's only by days. My discipler was 3 years old in Christ, but I've met people who were discipling others a week after they were baptized and had two or three weeks of training. Having no more than that, they're taking your spiritual life in their hands."

Eager to please their own disciplers, zealous new trainers tolerate no nonsense. Group members promoted to leadership may revel in their power and abuse it, but such power has its price. Rigorous enforcement of group rule not only demands compliant behavior from those beneath, but locks recruiters or trainers into serving as examples of perfection to those they control.

In the Boston Church of Christ, all rules and information flow from the top. This one-way communication stops dissent before it starts. Bob adds, "In a regular church, if you have questions you can go to your pastor, the pastor of another church, or one of the lay leaders. In the Boston Church of Christ, the only place you get the 'right' answers is from your discipler or from his discipler."

Tracy's experience with Scientology revealed the same rigidity, with the added ingredient of extremely ritualized communication designed to prevent discussion. "Basically you had one man who knew the truth, L. Ron Hubbard, and the rest of us were trying to learn the truth, so he called all the shots," she explains. "Hubbard was a crazy genius. Sometimes that craziness can be a teaching tool that really does work." In the case of Scientology, she found it didn't.

When Tracy first joined the Scientology staff, she helped with public relations. Next she was selected to spend a year of training in management and technical philosophy on the Mediterranean flagship where Hubbard lived. Throughout this time, she felt she was finding truth. "Many good things happened, and I felt my grasp on life and my personal abilities and powers were increased," she says. Back in Los Angeles after a short time, Tracy asked to work on Hubbard's ship. "To do that you had to sign a billion-year contract," she explains. "So I did that. I thought, this is it. I had found truth, so what's a billion years? I was planning on staying there, anyway."

As a ship staffer, Tracy was part of the inner circle, privy to information students and the public didn't know. Through diligent public relations efforts, Tracy built an organizationwide service to sell Scientology's psychological auditing and spiritual guidance. Yet she rarely saw the man in charge. "Hubbard stayed on the top level of the ship and he had a bunch of teenage girls as messengers," she explains. "If he wanted to talk to you, one of them would deliver his message.

You would speak to her, and she would take the reply back to him. Then she would return with his response." According to Tracy, the messengers, who were daughters of Scientologists, also spied on their fellow passengers to ferret out possible dissatisfaction or insubordination.

As in most dysfunctional religious groups, Scientologists were expected to follow orders precisely. When a messenger brought word that Tracy was to assign a critical piece of public relations work to someone she considered incompetent, she was upset. "This man was inept and unskilled," Tracy remembers. "He didn't understand the true value of Scientology. I couldn't understand why I was told to assign something to him; I knew it wouldn't work."

When members of dysfunctional religious groups are ordered to perform tasks that seem meaningless, wrong, or impossible to perform, they often rationalize away the ensuing conflict by telling themselves that they're being put through a loyalty test or that their leader is teaching them a lesson. Like children of an alcoholic who are told that Mom shrieks at them and beats them because she loves them, dysfunctional religious group members learn to tolerate contradictions and unpredictability. They are told that the development of this ability is part of their spiritual growth. When orders are meaningless, they believe their own lack of understanding to be the problem rather than recognizing escalating authoritarian abuse. Confronting members or leadership is seen as evidence of selfishness and egotism. Whether members are involved on a daily basis or urged to enter into communal living and sign over their money and worldly goods, they quickly learn that their time, thoughts, and feelings are not their own.

The desire for privacy is also considered a betrayal to the group, which refuses distinctions between members. In a such a group, failure to fuse is often grounds for punishment or excommunication rather than a step toward spiritual maturity.

In addition to being grilled about their thoughts and actions, dysfunctional religious group members find their relationships within the group monitored. In an invasion of intellectual privacy, attitudes are molded to fit the organization's norm. This is carried even further by leaders who claim to be able to read followers' minds. So, whether about money, time, thoughts or emotions, the motto of a severely dysfunctional religious group is "What's yours is mine."

Dysfunctional religious groups, where the teacher or leader is seen as a surrogate parent, have boundary violations similar to those of family incest. Boundaries may be blurred when a teacher shares inappropriate confidences about other students, lures a group member into emotional intimacy, or has sexual relations with a member. An incestuous parent may tell a child that the sexual attentions are good and special as well as threaten dire consequences for telling anyone. The authoritarian religious leader does the same. The ensuing shame and sense of despair and helplessness can be devastating. The very person to whom we have entrusted our souls has betrayed us by invading us at the deepest level. We come to believe that we cannot retain our bodily integrity and attain salvation or enlightenment.

While not happening in all religious groups, sexual abuse is quite common. The sexual exploits of television evangelists Jim Baker and Jimmy Swaggert came to national attention in recent years. The Tibetan Buddhist community in Boulder, Colorado, was left emotionally torn by the revelation that its spiritual head, who was infected with the AIDS virus, had knowingly spread the fatal disease to several students. In a survey by the United Methodist Church, 40 percent of women ministers said they had been victims of on-the-job sexual harassment that ranged from leers and inappropriate comments to rape.

During Anna's brief involvement as the student of a man claiming to be an enlightened spiritual teacher, she reports that he kissed her in front of other followers. He put his tongue in her mouth, tipped her over backward in a parody of a kiss from a 1940s movie, and held her there for several seconds. When Anna appeared flustered, he grinned and told her that he was trying to throw her off balance emotionally to advance her spiritual growth. She didn't believe him but felt flattered. It was just one more sign that she was the chosen one. After all, he had talked often in his lectures that his technique was to impregnate his female followers with enlightenment. Perhaps this kiss, she half believed, was part of the foreplay.

Brenda, too, was briefly involved with an incestuous group. The ongoing sexual abuse left her emotionally scarred. Four years after she left her primary teacher and his group, she went to a lecture given by another religious organization and began attending regular meetings. "My spiritual training from the last group made me look very good to them," she explains. "I knew things and was sensitive to things they didn't expect an average beginner to be sensitive to, so I was readily accepted into this group. I found out a lot, but it was all negative learning and very painful. I realized how easily I could be tricked by status, praise, and recognition. Give me status in a group, and I sell out. Part of the basis for their treatment of me was that the leader was attracted to me since I was amenable and flattered his ego."

Although Brenda never had sex with the leader, she came close. "Twelve of us in the group spent five to seven hours a night together, almost every night for a year, and we all hated each other," she says. "But the sexual energy in that room was intense. After the meetings, everybody was running around trying to seduce or to avoid being seduced by someone else. Finally a man was accused of rape by a female student who was the lover of the group's founder." This final incident caused her to leave without looking back, a move she has never regretted.

CHAPTER EIGHT

Dysfunctional Religious Family Dynamics II

In both dysfunctional families and religious groups, rigid boundaries and hierarchical authoritarian structures work only when group members comply with them. Since the emotional needs of individual members are not met in such systems, the potential for rebellion is high. So strategies develop to convince people that their needs do not deserve to be met and, in fact, people shouldn't have needs. Ironically, the needs that are denied are the very ones that may have originally prompted membership in the spiritual group. When individuals in unhealthy systems honor their own needs, they're seen as disloyal, sinful, or hateful—bad apples that may spoil the others. As such, individuals risk punishment or expulsion.

Dysfunctional systems that maintain a distorted reality insist on ultrarigid conformity, limit members' choices, and allow no questions or discussions. To avoid being punished or shunned, group members learn to stifle their feelings, to deny their perceptions, and to give away their power.

Unexpressed emotions don't disappear simply because they are declared illegal. Beneath the surface they still simmer, while any acting out is done against outsiders or comes out in heated rivalry and scapegoating among the rank and file.

Threats and Fear

Members of rigid religious organizations are controlled by a toxic combination of threats, shaming, and abuse. Disobedience and questioning are not tolerated, even though rules or beliefs may conflict with an individual member's conscience or search for truth. Such intimidation keeps members from testing their own limits or the group's boundaries.

Crystal says, "The church I belonged to teaches a lot of fear. They fear demons, and I was always full of fears and anxieties that I'd be taken by evil spirits. A great leader in the group works with her husband in casting out demons—they perform exorcisms. They visited our church, and even the highest authorities subjected themselves to that process." Crystal doubted that her emotional turmoil arose from the devil, suspecting instead that her childhood neglect and incest were the root of her problems. She refused to participate in an exorcism, afraid that the truth about her relationship with her father would be revealed and she would suffer humiliation in front of judgmental onlookers.

Sects often blame deviance from group norms on dark, supernatural powers. Their definition of satanic behavior can include anything from members questioning teachings and disobeying leaders, to associating with anyone outside the sect. The rituals are highly charged emotional spectacles involving exorcists who yell insults at the demons and press Bibles against the supposedly possessed person to burn the demon out. Other members who watch typically scream, cry, chant, and sing. Besides stamping out nonconformity, exorcisms are an all-purpose solution to any doubts or emotional problems a member might face.

In recovery from religious addiction, Crystal has begun changing the way she solves problems. "Life isn't always fair," she says. "Loved ones die, chaos and havoc occur, childhoods are troubled. Reality teaches you how to grieve. Sometimes the more pain I experience, the better I feel afterward." Her former refusal to cooperate in exorcisms, especially as a minister, set up an almost unbearable tension between herself and other group members. To avoid the ritual, she stuffed her feelings, hoping that her denial was strong enough to prevent being singled out.

"Holy terror" tactics are so effective that a member of a dysfunctional religious group has only to witness them once to decide to walk the straight and narrow. Bob says of his involvement with the Boston Church of Christ: "The group used shame to control people. Anything wrong is your fault; anything right is from God. However you were socialized, the Boston Church of Christ remolds you and spits you out. They impose their values and systems on you like parents do."

Tracy escaped punishment during her time as a Scientologist because the campaign she ran was extremely successful. Other Scientologists weren't so lucky. "If you asked questions, then you were sinful. Once you were assumed guilty, you were asked, What have you done? What sins have you committed? Finally you confessed to something, at which point they punished you."

Punishment included sleep deprivation and menial labor. "That's really a parent/child thing." Tracy says, "It was humiliating because it showed that you were a bad person. You ate beans and rice rather than steak and eggs. While I was in Scientology, I watched this fundamental discipline and control grow gradually. The organization I entered was very different from the organization I left."

To deter general disobedience and dissent in the members of dysfunctional religious groups, one member sometimes suffers extreme punishment or public humiliation. This rids the group of undesirables and reinforces the power structure. Writes Jerry Paul MacDonald, a University of Virginia researcher: "Excommunications succeed in deputizing a whole core of 'moral gatekeepers' who feel obligated to spy on one another and to mark those who exhibit questionable behavior." In studying people who had been expelled from a cult, he found that the process devastated and immobilized them psychologically. Some even expected to die from being cut off from the group.

Demand for Perfection

In unhealthy families, playing by the rules is equated with love. Similarly, religious groups that demand a high degree of compliance equate conformity with spiritual advancement. Perfection, rather than being something members work toward, is an immediate sign of a person's faith. To make mistakes is to fall sinfully away from the path of God rather than to be human. Under group pressure and frequently changing rules and expectations, fitting into the group culture means protection from criticism and shaming.

Only recently has Crystal begun to allow mistakes and to forgive herself for them. Her years in the charismatic, fundamentalist group taught her to act as if she were perfect to avoid abuse and the public shame of confession and exorcism. Her salvation depended on the level of perfection she could attain and on how well she performed.

"The church taught that if we could become perfect with God, we would be able to release the dead who are in bondage to corruption. In other words, the resurrection would come about," Crystal explains. "That made sense then, but I don't believe it anymore. I believe that God has put me here to mature as a human being. I have godly attributes because God is in me and I desire to be like the Divine, but I need to accept my humanity."

Crystal began to focus compulsively on outward appearance because the group judged her on that alone. The more she lived outside herself, concerned about what others thought of her, the less she was in touch with her own feelings. "My house had to be spotless and orderly," she says. "That was just part of my perfectionism, an image I protected in the church. I always had to be strong. Only in recovery have I been able to admit that I'm not perfect."

A dysfunctional religious group's demand for perfection condemns and judges members for things they cannot change. Within the context of the Unification Church, John felt that he was personally deficient. Like many people raised in dysfunctional homes, he had responded to the demand never to make mistakes by avoiding all risks. His life became constricted. "There was an extreme degree of pressure in the Unification Church to be perfect," he explains. "Reverend Moon is a perfect man, and our goal was to be a reflection of him and God. I became such a perfectionist that if I did not feel I could do something well, then I didn't try. Much of my potential was wasted because I feared I couldn't do things perfectly." In recovery John is contemplating changing jobs and returning to school. "Perfection is very dangerous and self-limiting," he says. "Letting go of the need to be perfect is a gift of sobriety."

Perfectionism is a way to cope with feelings of being inadequate, but group leaders can also use it to control and manipulate followers. Since perfection means being more than human, it is a goal that can never be fully attained. When seekers are told that they must be more than human to deserve God's love or the group's approval, they are doomed to fall short. Shame, then, becomes a constant companion.

Some New Age groups fall into the perfectionism trap when they insist that people are totally responsible for creating their reality. People who grew up in a dysfunctional family, they would say, chose the experience before they were born. The same applies to incest, alcoholism, domestic violence, and diseases like cancer or AIDS. The notion that if we are sincere in our beliefs, nothing unpleasant will ever happen to us, causes us to blame ourselves for things over which we may have no control.

After the perfection weapon is used against us, we feel wretched. Since we're isolated from outsiders, only the group is capable of alleviating our discomfort. When we are forgiven and embraced again, we find ourselves more tightly enmeshed in the dysfunctional system and grateful that someone, anyone, will tolerate us.

Like the child who is unpredictably beaten or verbally abused for simply existing, we place an extremely high value on words of praise, love, and acceptance from our parental group leaders. We may believe bad things happen only because we have made them happen. Like the child who thinks that Mom or Dad's drug addiction is her fault, we brood over how things would be if we were just better people, and we try harder to avoid making mistakes that will incur the wrath of our superiors.

Don't Question

People who ask questions or express doubts threaten the group's cohesiveness and are discouraged or suppressed. It takes only one or two questions for a quizzical member to realize that suppressing doubts is better than voicing them. Bob discovered that mindlessly following the leader is dangerous, but also extremely tempting at times. "When people follow and don't think, there's a strong potential for psychological and even physical damage because people don't fight back," he says. "I thought I was having fun. They validate you and emphasize love to keep you. If you do ask questions, they remove that reinforcement. You are ignored or told you were sinning. Every group has a mechanism for dealing with doubt. The Hare Krishnas chant; in the Boston Church of Christ people pray very hard when doubts come up, or they ask somebody who tells them the doubts come from Satan."

As in a dysfunctional family, once cracks appear in our certainty that an isolated and dictatorial unit is the only shape a group can assume, the floodgates of doubt open up. Other beliefs and assumptions come under question, and members respond by trying to change the system. Outnumbered and overpowered, however, in the end they either reform themselves to fit the group or leave.

When Tracy was ordered to hand her public relations project over to a Scientology member she believed was incompetent, she rebelled. "I decided to do it myself because I wanted it done right," she says. No sooner had she begun than a messenger told her that Hubbard wanted to know if she had delegated the task. Tracy said she had carefully examined the situation and determined that she could do a better job.

"I thought making my own decisions was good, because that's what the training had taught me," she says. "The messenger returned and said LRH was furious and wanted to know what evidence I had for my decision. I said, 'I know I can do a better job!' LRH told me not to act on my knowledge. That floored me. Why were we learning to raise our capability if were not supposed to use it?" Instead of suppressing doubts about the contradictions, she followed her instincts.

In open defiance of her orders, Tracy executed a highly successful campaign and earned the organization a great deal of money. Because she had challenged authority and won, exercised critical thinking and reclaimed power over her own life, her success was a turning point for her. "I never forgot that incident," she says. "I felt my trust had been betrayed." Nevertheless, for many months afterward, she kept her questions and feelings to herself.

Don't Feel Your Feelings

Stuffing feelings for prolonged periods causes people to disconnect from their emotions and identity. Feelings provide clues to our needs, but in a restrictive and controlled group, we become numb to our feelings to survive. A natural consequence is to allow damaging involvement to continue. We're frightened to move away from the group because we have no clue about what to move toward.

Explains Bob: "The greatest damage the Boston Church of Christ does is psychological. Some people in the campus ministry had the potential to be harmed. For example, one person was very shy and took a long time to be converted. He couldn't be baptized, so he wasn't considered a Christian." Even though the group and individuals cut themselves off from their feelings, their emotions still ferment below the surface.

Intense Membership Rivalry

People place a high value on any commodity that is scarce. When dysfunctional religious groups are run by a charismatic leader and the members crave attention, the elevated person's favor becomes a commodity to be heatedly vied for. Depending on the group's belief system, even God's love may have to be earned by strict adherence to the group's rules. Under these circumstances, members become polarized and highly competitive. A group may give the appearance of practicing brotherly love, but underneath members sabotage one another and jockey for position in the contest for God's favor. This cutthroat way of relating is justified religiously.

In the Unification Church, John was unprepared for the intense rivalry he experienced. He witnessed heated and hateful interactions between spiritual brothers and sisters fighting to get close to the leader. John says, "The closer you were to the top, the harder you sought Reverend Moon's approval by trying to complete your mission. The higher the stakes, the more eager you were to please. Eternal life, spiritual life, those are high stakes. But you would do whatever it took to get the job done, even sacrifice someone's health. If it meant sacrificing someone's health or spiritual life, then that was the price you paid for eternal life."

In competition of this nature, avoiding the harsh judgments of fellow members takes precedence over individuals' relationship with God. John explains, "It was hard. I didn't feel judged by Reverend Moon or God, but when I didn't sell all my fund-raising candy, I felt judged by the brothers and sisters. Fingers pointed when I stood up because I couldn't sit in the prayer position for another minute. I was seen as deficient."

During John's tenure with the group, he saw squabbles develop along international lines. "Korean members disliked Japanese members because Japan had subjugated Korea for so long," John explains. "But the Koreans felt superior because Moon is Korean. Some of the Japanese believed they were a superior race. The Americans were considered spoiled Westerners who didn't know anything. The group dynamics caused a lot of pain."

Scapegoating

Suppressed anger and sibling rivalry eventually cause one or more members of the group to be scapegoated. Like the scapegoat in a dysfunctional family, these people haven't necessarily violated the group's rules, but they are either blamed for all the group's problems or they serve as a diversion from those problems.

According to the teachings of the Holy Order of Mans, anger had to be transcended before a person could become more holy. "I was the shadow, a scapegoat for the order," says Anna. "In our group, one woman was more of a scapegoat than I was, and everybody projected their anger onto her. She couldn't keep a job, she was always physically in pain, and she had no money. I was the victim, she was the crazy. Whenever I did anything to pull out of the victim stance, they put me back in my place. Yet we all professed brotherly love."

Anger that didn't get projected onto other group members got stored. Anna concludes, "Where did the anger go? Nowhere! Once everybody left the safety in the Holy Order of Mans, we still had to deal with who we were and all of the things that for seven years we had all denied."

Denial

Dysfunctional religious groups have forbidden questions, so they end up with many group secrets. Secrets are closely guarded, and conflicts, instead of being resolved, are internalized and eventually solidify into a heavy burden of emotional pain.

Tracy says, "There were secrets in Scientology that you couldn't talk about. I disobeyed orders and became successful. Ironically, my success allowed me further into the inner circle. There I began to know about high-level decisions in this network of worldwide management. Some things really disturbed me; for instance, we had infiltrated the IRS and had blackmailed people. That went against some of the teachings, but, even more than that, it went against my personal values." Even though she was let in on the secrets, Tracy felt reluctant to blow the whistle or leave the group until the following year.

John, too, was wounded by his group's denial. The longer he stayed in the Unification Church, the closer he came to the ultimate goal of being blessed by Reverend Moon and marrying a woman selected by the organization. His homosexuality, however, posed an immediate conflict. "I could live without sex, but I couldn't live with a woman," he says. "I knew I couldn't change, and I felt ashamed and guilty. But today I'm angry at the group for creating a situation that was the same as growing up in Texas. My mom, stepdad, and I lived in this small house and I would come home tripping on acid. Nothing was ever said. If we don't speak the words, then we can pretend problems don't exist."

The issues families and religious groups don't talk about can imply more stringent judgments than those things openly condemned. If a particular behavior is too bad to be spoken about, the shame attached to it becomes unbearable. In the Unification Church, to speak openly about sex was forbidden. Instead, members referred to it as a Chapter Three problem. The *Chapter Three* they referred to was the Genesis account of the fall of man. "That's how antiseptic it became," John comments. "If a brother and sister had Chapter Three problems, they needed to be separated. I don't think the word *homosexuality* was ever spoken. There were some brothers I might have been able to confide in, but I believed their response would be: 'That happened before you were reborn. Pray about it.'" Although John left the group nearly ten years ago, he still feels a great deal of guilt and shame.

Like the scars left by a dysfunctional family, the psychological and spiritual wounds inflicted by a dysfunctional religious group can be long-lasting. To survive, members learn to deny their feelings and values and fear that they cannot exist without the group. *Violated* and *raped* are words former members often use to describe the aftermath of betrayal and anger when they realize they have bonded with an abusive religious group.

Even though the distorted mind-set and behavior patterns we shared with other members are no longer necessary after leaving the group, we cannot easily give them up. Not only have we learned to mistrust our perceptions of reality, but our integrity and sense of self was subverted at the hands of a parental religious figure to whom we granted trust and devotion.

CHAPTER NINE

False Prophets—Men of God, Feet of Clay

A dervish was traveling down the road one day when he spied a horrible, hairy demon resting beneath a tree. "Why aren't you out causing trouble?" the dervish stopped to ask the demon. "Isn't that what you devils are supposed to do?"

The demon shook his ugly head, a tear pooling in the corner of his red eye. Sadly he replied, "There are so many theologians, philosophers, and teachers who claim to be able to lead people along the path that I have nothing left to do."

Finding a good spiritual mentor is not easy. The false prophets discussed in the Bible were an issue long before the scriptures were written. At best, self-proclaimed men of God only temporarily divert us from our spiritual growth process. At worst they encourage us to worship them and then betray our trust.

"The teacher is a shepherd and his flock is the people. He has to help and save them, not exploit and destroy them. Is the shepherd there for the flock, or is the flock there for the shepherd?" asked Jami, a Sufi poet who lived in the 1400s. About a hundred years later, the Christian mystic Saint John of the Cross wrote, "Some confessors and spiritual directors, because they have no perception or experience of these ways, are a hindrance and an evil, rather than a help to souls;

they are like the builders of Babel, who, when required to furnish certain materials, furnished others of a very different sort because they knew not the language of those around them, and thus the building was stopped."

It is easier to discern helpful teachers from the harmful ones in retrospect rather than during interactions with them. Clearly, Jim Jones was a false prophet, but until the end most of his followers were convinced he knew something they didn't, and only he was capable of teaching it to them.

Not only do certain ministers and spiritual teachers have personal charisma that attracts and binds us to them, but they may possess numinous qualities most of us do not encounter in everyday life. When we're in their presence, we feel differently than when we're around other people. Often, that feeling is difficult to put into words.

To complicate matters, we may question feelings of uneasiness when they arise. If we were capable of judging, we tell ourselves, then we wouldn't have sought out a teacher. After all, if we were taking an algebra class, we'd have to trust the math teacher and follow that person's directions, or we'd never learn how to work binomial equations. Being a serious student implies trusting that the teacher will help us learn. There are times we simply must suspend judgment, times when critical questions are rude and actually detract from the learning process.

If the teacher is from another culture or spiritual tradition, we may lack a frame of reference for evaluation. We may be confused about that person's intent or ability to impart knowledge. This is often true with religious leaders who claim to be enlightened masters who can transmit knowledge without language. If all we've ever experienced are the sermons and handshakes from the neighborhood pastor, the exotic atmosphere surrounding a guru can be seductive.

Holy Man or Devil's Disciple?

When we meet an enlightened teacher, it is tempting to suspend all judgment and disbelief. It is also tempting to elevate anyone who makes us feel different to the status of enlightened master. We fail to distinguish that many types of spiritual teachers exist—from those who deceive us for personal gain to those teachers who are truly filled with spiritual light. In the introduction to their book *Spiritual Choices: The Problem of Recognizing Authentic Paths to Inner Transformation*, Ken Wilbur, Dick Anthony, and Bruce Ecker list four kinds of people who may appear to be spiritual teachers.

False guides who practice deceit and hypocrisy often stage occurrences that followers interpret as miraculous. Using the techniques of stage magicians, they may pretend to read minds or to heal followers. Their charisma is purely psychological. Their power is the result of calculation and manipulation. Oftentimes, it is less difficult to see behind the facade of these pseudo-gurus.

The more dangerous spiritual guide or teacher has attained a certain level of spiritual transcendence. Through spiritual practice or mystical experience they have obtained extraordinary knowledge, power, and personal qualities. Although traditional psychological literature denies the existence of spiritual psychic abilities, religious writings and transpersonal psychologists confirm the phenomenon. Despite their heightened psychic abilities and insights, these teachers lack the ability to move beyond egotism and personal desires. They may be self-deluded, or they may deliberately use their increased powers to control others.

The last two types of spiritual mentors—the advanced guide and the fully enlightened guide—are able to move beyond personal desires and self-delusion. Wilbur, Anthony, and Ecker believe that the advanced guide's mind encompasses other minds but is not consciously one with the Infinite Mind. The fully enlightened guide is one with all beings on all levels of consciousness. In addition, he or she is conscious of being the true nature of matter, energy, and mind. Obviously, teachers at this level are not an easy find.

Miracle Makers and Pseudo-Gurus

One day a long, long time ago, two Zen disciples were arguing about the relative merits of their respective masters. Said the first student, "My master is wonderful. You really must study under him. The work he does is awesome."

"Just what does he do?" asked the second student.

"Why, he performs miracles!" replied the first student.

Miracles?" The other sounded skeptical.

The first student dashed away to fetch his master, who stood on the shore of a lake, chanting and hopping alternately on one foot, then the other. Two hours later, he tentatively stepped onto the surface of the water, which held him up. Slowly, he made his way across the lake, reaching the distant shore just as the sun was setting.

"See?" boasted the first student. "My Zen master is better than yours. Can yours walk on water?"

"Why would he want to do that?" asked the other." For a quarter he could hire a boat to ferry him to the other side in five minutes!"

Miracles, while impressive, can dazzle unsuspecting observers into following a teacher away from God and into the realm of idol worship. Thomas Merton, Catholic contemplative and student of Zen, wrote, "The most dangerous man in the world is the contemplative who is guided by nobody. He trusts his own visions. He obeys the attractions of an interior voice but will not listen to other men. He identifies the will of God with anything that makes him feel within his own heart a big, warm, sweet interior glow. The sweeter and warmer the feeling, the more he is convinced of his infallibility. And if the sheer force of his own self-confidence communicates itself to other people and gives them the impression that he really is a saint, such a man can wreck a whole city, religious order, or even a nation. The world is covered with scars that have been left in its flesh by visionaries like these."

Many people who meditate regularly experience the warm glow Merton mentioned, as well as heightened sensory awareness. Sounds may seem clearer and colors more luminous. Things outside the realm of ordinary experiences may begin to happen. You know the phone is going to ring before it does, or you know who is calling before you pick up the receiver. You are closely attuned to people's thoughts. Kundalini energy may rise inside you like a ball of fire moving up your spine. If you belong to a meditation group or shamanic drumming group, to your utter amazement, you may discover that you and other members have shared dreams.

Although such phenomena have been ignored or scoffed at by the Western psychological community, they are accepted facts of life in both Eastern and Western mystical traditions and are long-acknowledged side results of meditating, praying, or fasting. Because Western mysticism has been traditionally confined to monasteries and convents and because traditional psychologists often refuse to acknowledge these events, they seem alien to us.

But they do happen. According to Catholic sociologist Andrew Greeley, 40 percent of Americans have had a mystical experience. Far from being supernatural, these experiences are a natural part of spiritual life. Although we may credit a teacher or guru for giving them to us, they probably would occur anyway, triggered by events that alter our consciousness, such as chanting, fasting, dancing, drumming, praying, and meditating. Such consciousness-altering practices have been an integral part of mystical tradition for thousands of years.

Providing Meaning for the Mystery

Experience in a particular spiritual group helps us interpret internal transcendent events. Most of the people I interviewed for this book had mystical experiences when they belonged to dysfunctional religious groups. Even though they no longer feel the groups are valid or spiritual, they still believe in the luminosity and personal meaning of their mystical experiences.

Whether the experiences happen during private meditation or in the presence of a spiritual teacher, we may become overwhelmed by them. Because society, and especially the scientific community, view such experiences as hallucinatory products of imagination, we may have no one to discuss them with outside our chosen group. To be honest would invite being labeled emotionally disturbed, so we keep our experiences secret. They may then become supercharged, sometimes with false meaning.

Even if our mentor does not distort or impose a manipulatory meaning on our experiences, we may interpret them to mean more than they do. Without balance and discrimination, we make these psychic events more than milestones on the way to union with God or states to be passed through. We make them goals in their own right, greedily seeking them out as an addict would seek out a drug. We may develop a relationship with the person we believe can give us these feelings, much as an addict would the person who supplied the drugs.

It is easy to see how someone, touched by the mystery available to us all, could mistake these temporary bursts of illumination for enlightenment and set out on a mission to save the world. Without the guidance provided by a trained and credential spiritual director, as Thomas Merton describes, it is difficult to delude oneself about saving the world.

Even though mystical experiences may deepen understanding, provide insight, and enhance creativity, they do not necessarily change a self-styled teacher's personality or character. Mystical experiences are not the same as enlightenment, and they do not always lead to enlightened action. One Indian anthropologist remarked that a person who is a stinker before a mystical experience will be a stinker after the experience, too.

Swiss psychologist Carl Jung also addressed this issue. He termed the inflated sense of having superpowers because of a mystical experience a *mana* personality. *Mana*, in Polynesian, means "a magical power that enables one to perform miracles." Along with *mana* comes an intense sense of mission. Writes Jungian psychologist June Singer in *Seeing Through the Visible World,* "These people project charisma, that magical personal quality of leadership that arouses enthusiasm and popular support. As long as the individual who is gripped by the *mana* personality archetype believes that the power belongs to him or her, the situation can be more hazardous than wildfire."

The *mana* archetypes that drive some spiritual leaders cannot be limited to misguided gurus of Eastern religious traditions based on meditation. Charismatic Christianity, with its "gifts of the Spirit" that may include speaking in tongues and prophesy, offers many opportunities for mystical experiences, too. It can provide a setting for psychologically troubled people to have a sudden flash of euphoria, or to develop the charisma to attract followers and become psychologically troubled religious autocrats. New Age practitioners also may be characterized by this archetype.

The Making of a Master Manipulator

In some cases a traumatic life event serves as the catalyst for charisma. For example, in shamanism the healer, or shaman, is usually a wounded healer, someone who has faced death, either symbolically or actually, and lived. This experience spiritually empowers the survivor. Many charismatic leaders of dysfunctional religious groups have had similar experiences. The Reverend Sun Myung Moon had intense mystical visions beginning at age 16, but not until he was a political prisoner in Korea did he synthesize The Divine Principal. Scientology's founder, L. Ron Hubbard, served in the Pacific in World War II and was seriously wounded. During his year-long hospital recovery, he became charged with his mission and pulled together the basic tenets of Scientology.

Researchers have yet to typify a dysfunctional religious leader personality, but pseudo-gurus do share some characteristics:

◆ They promise followers salvation or enlightenment.
◆ They are driven by an intense sense of mission.
◆ They often feel called by God.
◆ Many have extremely high self-regard, sometimes bordering on megalomania.
◆ They control and manipulate others without remorse, believing the end justifies the means.

Feelings of alienation from society existed long before they form their groups. They view followers as things or objects rather than human beings with souls and easily sacrifice them for the cause.

Such a person usually finds that forming an organization is a fairly easy task to accomplish. All it requires is to gather a grouping of disciples who can be convinced that the leader is uniquely qualified to teach them. Once the leader has assembled the pupils, there are numerous ways to establish and reinforce authority. Members can be rewarded or coerced. Attention can be selectively given and then withheld. Ritualized contact with students helps formalize the dysfunctional group leader's power. Keeping oneself isolated from followers makes one appear special. Developing unique speech patterns, dressing unusually, and acting in unpredictable ways keeps students off balance and in line.

Some leaders are masters at psychological manipulation rather than spiritual mastery, even though they may express a strong disagreement with psychology. They are experts at sensing discomfort and disillusionment and at alleviating it. They are keenly perceptive about unspoken yearnings and can voice them, causing others to mistakenly believe they are able to read minds.

Eye contact, gestures, facial expressions, and pacing surround the leader with a sense of power. Relying on rapport, they create a sense of identity and shared experience. When we are with them, we feel at one with them. That sense of oneness can be enhanced through altered states of consciousness. The ability to put people into trancelike states is relatively simple to develop. A voice roll, a patterned and rhythmic way of speaking, and the right lighting contribute to leaving us spellbound.

Spellbound

For recovering dependents and codependents, charismatic leaders may have an even more spellbinding effect. When a religious teacher or minister moves rapidly toward intimacy, we interpret the chill of this inappropriate closeness as a spiritual experience. We may mistake the thrill of fear that comes from boundary invasion for arousal or attraction. The fear/attraction conflict set up by the inappropriate intimacy is exploited by a manipulative leader. Since dependent people are used to having their boundaries invaded, they are slow to pull away from emotional and spiritual violators. What should serve as a warning sign serves instead as a lure.

Anna's first spiritual mentor in the Holy Order of Mans was positive for her, and she still values the experience. She explains, "By experiencing a teacher's energy, you do have an opportunity to open up, and it's very valid." A more recent encounter with a teacher who claimed to be an enlightened master was far different. "He said it was his job to impregnate the women around him with an infusion of his energy," she says. "He kept saying to me, 'Why don't you wake up and be with the big boys. Your next step is to be illumined; your next step is to be infused with the great ball of light.'"

Her new teacher told her that he recognized her as one of his advanced helpers and asked if she recognized him. When that didn't sway her, he increased the intimacy quotient, telling her that the two of them had been lovers in a past life. For a time this closeness aroused Anna, but it was the intimacy that felt incestuous and coercive. "It makes you feel like a little girl," she says. "You want the unconditional love, and you'll do almost anything to get it."

Her experiences have caused her to distrust the euphoric and sometimes sexual energy that charismatic leaders project. "Over the last fifteen years of meeting several teachers who have set themselves up as gurus," she says, "I believe the real teachers are the ones who don't go about it with a whole lot of hoopla, the people who are just *being* what they teach—no public relations jobs. They're the people who go quietly about being light in the world, and only those who have the sight to see can see it."

Brenda agrees: "I deeply respect my former spiritual teacher. He is a good man, and for me right now that is a higher compliment than saying somebody is enlightened. A good person is incredible, and I don't mean Christ on the Cross. I just mean he is honorable and can be trusted."

Look for spiritual leaders and teachers who

♦ encourage you to form and verbalize your own opinions.

♦ make you take responsibility for your spiritual growth.

♦ foster your acceptance of yourself as a flawed human being, rather than demanding unattainable perfection.

♦ acknowledge that your relationship with God and care for yourself take primacy over a relationship with a spiritual teacher.

♦ don't confuse enslavement with devotion or surrender.

♦ empower you to make wise choices.

♦ seem worthy of your trust and allow you to take your time trusting.

♦ help you feel good about your spiritual development rather than overly enamored with them.

♦ help you outgrow them rather than encourage ongoing dependence.

Follow the Leader

Even with all the charisma and manipulative power in the world, if leaders don't have willing followers, they don't have a group to spearhead. Religious teachers and leaders—ethical and growth-promoting ones and dishonest ones—rely on the power followers give them.

Rather than discouraging the tendency of followers to deify a spiritual mentor, dysfunctional leaders cultivate it by making themselves seem more mysterious. Just as we project larger-than-life qualities onto movie stars, we do the same to the guru we adore. When affiliated with a superhuman guru or charismatic minister, we may see ourselves in a better light. Generally, the more we dislike ourselves, the more we will attach to these people until, rather than God, they become our objects of worship.

Tracy explains how she felt about the reclusive L. Ron Hubbard, whom she seldom saw even when she lived aboard his ship. "Only five or six hundred people ever met Hubbard, so you could project on that mystery anything you wanted to. I projected complete enlightenment into the vacuum—somebody who knew the answer to everything."

She continues, "He was almost a god to me until I met him, then I had a hard time maintaining that projection. But I found a way to explain things that didn't make sense; if a god does something questionable, you tell yourself there's something wrong with your mind, or you're spiritually defective and you try harder. We told ourselves for years that LRH couldn't possibly know about the illegal stuff going on, or he'd be angry. I don't believe that anymore. He knew what was going on the whole time."

The Need to Please

People's tendency to please authority figures rather than protest or go their own way isn't unique to spiritual groups. A few years ago a Yale-based psychological researcher named Stanley Milgram discovered that people are willing not only to experience discomfort themselves, but will inflict it obediently on others if instructed to by an authority figure. To prove his theory, Milgram recruited people to assist him. He recruited some volunteers to act as helpers and to question research subjects. If the subjects answered incorrectly, the helpers were to shock them by administering 195 to 300 volts of electricity to them by way of electrodes attached to their bodies.

Unknown to the recruited helpers, no real shocks were given. But when the helpers pressed the buttons, subjects yelled, screamed, writhed, and twitched very convincingly. Despite the possible consequences, the helpers were willing to administer pain to other people simply because a researcher wearing a white lab coat had told them to do so. Rather than displease an authority figure, the helpers would, in effect, torture people, even though such acts violated their values and caused them to shake, sweat, stutter, and show other signs of extreme psychological discomfort.

Obedience to authority, especially religious authority, is something many of us have been consciously schooled in all our lives. Even mainstream religions often do not reward questioning and critical thinking, but instead encourage members to passively follow the leader. Says Tracy, who was Catholic before she became a Scientologist, "I have a theory that traditional religion sets us up for dysfunctional religious groups. In the Catholic church, the priests have the only pipeline to God. You're not allowed to have your own pipeline; everything is approved by the Pope in this hierarchy. It's the same system in Scientology. All you do is replace one father figure with another. Rather than God, we had LRH; rather than priests, we had 14-year-old girls running messages around. I'd been learning to play that game from birth."

The Santa Claus God

Sometimes the childhood desire for a perfect parent leads an adult into a relationship with a spiritual teacher. Maharaj Ji, the founder of The Divine Light Mission, was considered to *be* God, a big attraction for Gary. "I always figured Santa and God must be the same guy because both have all the same powers," Gary says. "Omnipotence, omnipresence, the ability to slide down a billion chimneys in an hour, those things take magical powers. At 6 or 7, I had this pretty firm idea I called the 'Santa Claus God.' When you find out your spiritual teacher is really just a mixed-up man, your concept of God starts to change."

Although Gary has no doubt that much of what happened in the Divine Light Mission was dysfunctional, he does question how much of his subservience and conformity was because of this master. "I really listened," says Gary. "Occasionally he'd say something in public that wasn't transmitted through the bureaucracy. He once said, 'This isn't a religion and I'm not God. I'm your teacher. I grew up in schools where the teachers were called *master* and I thought that's what they meant when they called me Perfect Master. Like a mathematics master or a geography master, I'm in charge of the perfect.' Immediately the bureaucracy said he didn't mean that; he's pure and perfect, and we were to do as we were told. My concept of God and the Divine has changed from the Santa Claus superhero image."

Total Trust

Brenda found her relationship with her teacher to be profoundly determined by her early conditioning. "In my childhood I learned to trust no one. It was natural that I would completely adore the first person I believed I could trust."

She further reflects, "I think of the little children thing of Christ except you enter as little children. Little children are imitative and devoted to their role models. You can't even enter the door of mathematics or auto mechanics without some of that. Maybe the problem is that we only allow ourselves to be totally filled with admiration once or twice in our whole lives. If devotion was an easy thing for us to do, then we wouldn't have the problem. When we only fall at one person's feet, we fall hard."

Since living spiritual teachers are not a part of Western culture, we can't look around us for models of healthy devotion. Instead, we are forced to invent our own. If we were raised in an unhealthy family, then, like Brenda, we reenact what we learned as children. Only after Brenda left the group did she come to realize that her teacher was a human being and that if he didn't completely fuse with her, she was still fine as a person. "That was the neurotic part," she confesses. "I needed his complete attention. I believed that I had to revere the things that he did and reject anything he didn't like. I needed his complete attention. I couldn't accept that he simply wasn't interested in my interests. I couldn't hear it that way. I heard it as 'God doesn't love me anymore,' and I left. He was being himself and I wanted him to be God."

She concludes, "Maybe idolatry was a necessary step on the spiritual ladder. You're existentially disappointed if you believe in an idol because the idol is not God. My spiritual path demanded that I learn that. Sometimes to grow spiritually, you have to put everything on the line and be willing to be burned for it. If you're unwilling to surrender and be hurt sometimes, you're not going to go where you want to go."

Devotion or Love Addiction?

Devotion, surrender, and charisma can be a volatile mix even under the best of circumstances. An unhealed spiritual leader may inflict wounds on followers in much the same way shame is handed down in dysfunctional families. When spiritual students do not address the emotional healing process but look to a guru or a minister for validation and self-worth, a growth-crippling pattern of codependency and love addiction can occur. The more we like ourselves and rely on our inner guidance, the more likely we are to find a growth-promoting teacher with whom we can develop a good relationship. In the words of the Taoist philosopher Chuang Tzu, "If one is true to one's Self and follows its teaching, who need be without a teacher?"

Love Addiction or Devotion?

The following are strong indications that our relationship with a spiritual teacher or leader is unhealthy:

♦ Instead of loving from our hearts, we expect our teacher's love to fill our empty spaces.

♦ Because we cannot love ourselves, we focus our attention on getting our leader to love us more.

♦ When we have no spiritual leader, we panic instead of working on our growth.

♦ We try to protect ourselves from our teacher because we feel fearful and vulnerable, yet we stay in the relationship and pretend nothing is wrong.

♦ The leader seems to be our missing half.

♦ Instead of feeling comforted and peaceful in the presence of the teacher, we feel anxious or angry.

♦ The longer we stay with this teacher, the more our fear and dependency increase.

♦ Without the teacher, we fear spiritual or emotional destruction.

♦ Rather than broadening our horizons and interests, our relationship with the teacher dramatically narrows them.

♦ We think obsessively about the teacher, have imaginary conversations, and are unable to focus on other parts of our lives.

♦ Our friends, values, and interests drop away or change as we become more involved with the leader or the group.

If you recognized yourself in the list you just read, take heart, you are not alone. You can trust your feelings to guide you as you move to leave behind a distinctive religious involvement. You may feel disappointment and grief for awhile, but you will soon discover that freedom, joy and peace are by-products of true spiritual growth.

CHAPTER TEN

Trouble in Paradise— Breaking Free

Recovery from religious abuse can be a slow process. The decision to leave a dysfunctional religious group can be agonizing. As members become aware of the difference between their organization's teachings and its practices, their trust in its integrity begins to erode.

Generally this loss of trust leads to anguish characterized by feelings of ambivalence and denial. People grappling with the decision to leave an abusive religious group may protect themselves by presenting a calm, devoted facade to the leader and to their peers, a deception that usually causes them even more emotional discomfort.

Some believers remain in the group for months after realizing their need to leave. They wrestle with the fear that, if they defect, they will be eternally condemned, a fear often reinforced by the group's teachings. Others worry about their physical and mental well-being.

Being cast out of the garden may provoke extreme anxiety if the group has met all of a member's needs for food, clothing, housing, and friendship. The prospect of starting life over with no assets and with few or no friends is indeed daunting. After investing so much time, energy, and money into a religious group, it is difficult to admit that doing so was wrong. Often, the bigger the investment, the stronger the interest in hanging on.

After the initial disenchantment, survivors sometimes attempt to resolve conflict with the group by rededicating themselves to its mission. They tell themselves that they are unworthy, sinful, or stupid— messages they often first heard in childhood.

When self-blame and renewed commitment fail, people may simply want for conflicts to resolve themselves. They may also cling to the illusion that they can change the system from the inside, convincing others to see the light and save themselves from spiritual domination. For a while, their mission to save others may distract them from their own inner turmoil.

Even after they separate physically from a dysfunctional religious group, they may remain emotionally dependent. Most people who leave such groups, willfully or otherwise, feel uprooted and lost. Anger, depression, confusion, and betrayal alternate with the shame of having invested in the group.

Tracy: Facing Fear

As Tracy rose higher in Scientology circles and discovered more about the group's illegal activities, her dedication wavered. "I didn't object to the teachings," she explains. "I was beginning to see that the organization, and even L. Ron Hubbard, didn't follow them. It took a year to decide whether I was going to live by my own values or someone else's."

Tracy's fear of leaving was increased by stories that fellow Scientologists might force her to remain in the group or kill her if she left. "If you said you were leaving or spoke against the church, you were locked in a room and browbeaten until you confessed that you were wrong," she says. "I didn't want to go through that."

Anxiety about the threat of abuse paled next to her terror of being cut off from the belief system she had assumed was her only route to salvation. "If you were denied Scientology, you would never find eternal bliss or enlightenment," she explains. "To me, that meant hell. Scientology controlled you through fear." Tracy decided that if she confronted the organization and got through the worst, her fears would cease.

Today she compares her feelings during that time to those of a battered woman coping with the unpredictability of her situation. "If I was going to be banned forever, I figured I might as well get it over with. I was tired of living in fear, and I wanted it to end." Secretly she made plans to escape.

Married by that time to a man in the group, Tracy kept her intentions secret from her husband, Sam, until the night before they were to depart for a two-week vacation to visit Tracy's parents. Only then did she reveal her plan to pack all her belongings and never return. Sam decided to leave with Tracy. Choosing to leave together, they smuggled everything they owned into their car.

Only when they were far away did Tracy call headquarters to say she no longer wanted to be a Scientologist. "They kicked us out and declared that no one in Scientology could speak to us," she recounts. "This was a very heavy thing because I'd spent seven years with them and didn't have a friend in the world who wasn't in the group. We were completely ostracized."

Life outside the group presented another set of problems. For seven years Tracy had worked for 13 dollars a week, just enough to cover necessities. With only 20 dollars to her name, Tracy had no idea how to open a checking account or apply for a credit card. "I'd lived a cloistered life," she says. "Money is another control mechanism; you never have any money, so you can't go anywhere unless somebody helps you." Tracy and Sam had no choice but to move in with Tracy's parents.

Another problem arose for the couple. Tracy suspected that Sam had gone along with her decision to leave only to keep her happy. He was, in fact, bitter, and his resentment became a burden. At times, she felt superior to Sam because he hadn't seen the truth about Scientology on his own. Their marriage began to suffer.

Tracy's first years outside the organization were marked by carefully crafted deceptions in all areas of her life. "I was scared to death the group members were going to kill me," she says. "I didn't want them to know where I was." She lied on her first job applications when asked where she had worked for the previous seven years. After supervising sixty workers in a multi-million-dollar organization whose income averaged $400,000 a week, Tracy found herself working for little more than minimum wage.

She limited her friendships to former Scientologists and avoided spirituality of any sort. "I wanted to live normally," she says. "That meant staying married, holding a job, buying a house in the suburbs, watching TV, going to football games, and drinking beer. I had never drunk before, but I started." Finally, she told herself, "I am not going to live in denial. I am interested in continuing my spiritual quest."

Renee: Choosing Hell

Like Tracy, Renee had few doubts about the wisdom of continued affiliation with her convent until she entered its inner circle. By then she had been a nun for ten years, time enough to heal from childhood wounds.

Teaching first grade had delighted her. She had also studied theology and philosophy. When she occasionally questioned the order's theology, she blamed her questions on youth and ignorance and took another class, certain that someday she would gain understanding. She describes herself as a "happy little nun who didn't rock the boat."

That changed in her late twenties, when she was put in charge of instructing novices. Expected to provide explanations, Renee suddenly realized that she had no answers. And she would not teach what she did not know or believe. The doubts she had kept hidden away for years began to surface.

She tried to deal with her doubts by attending an intensive twelve-week workshop during which she lived on the grounds of a state hospital and did pastoral counseling on the wards. She met with a therapist three times a week. The effect of this work was unsettling. "For six weeks I didn't talk in the therapy group because I wasn't used to expressing feelings," she says. "I was used to going into my little cell and talking to God, who was *out there*." At the end of the workshop, she asked to be transferred to Boston for two years to study for a Master of Divinity degree.

During those two years, she realized she had outgrown her faith. "After fifteen years, I knew my professors didn't know any more than I did," she explains. "If you want to be a spokesperson for Catholicism, you have to accept the whole package, logical or not. A lot of it does make sense. Even so, something dies in people who stay because they fear they can't survive outside. Creativity, curiosity, the joy of living fully are killed by compromises made in fear."

Renee spent her last two years in the order in a nearly constant struggle to resolve her spiritual crisis. Every paper she wrote touched on her personal dilemma. By the time she left the university, she was certain she had made the right choice.

She says. "I remember thinking if God is a giant CPA in the sky keeping tabs on people or if He is a mad scientist, then the world doesn't make much sense, and I choose to go to hell. When I left the convent, I chose hell, because I was choosing my own pain and choosing to become responsible for myself. I didn't know what life would be like because I had grown up in a system that told you about the world in a judgmental way. Most religions tell their members they're more spiritually advanced than other people; it keeps them separate. Nuns are even more separate."

Although the women she had lived with for years didn't shun her after she left the order, they could not understand why she had broken her vows. "Those still in the order didn't want to hear too much; they were frightened," she reflects. "They ask themselves, 'Am I stupid to stay?' To not persevere means you're an eternal failure. By that time, though, I believed change was okay."

Bob: Ticket to Heaven

Bob's abrupt departure from the Boston Church of Christ was engineered by his father, so Bob didn't live through a period of ambivalence before making the break. He did, however, find himself drawn to return to the group after he had received exit counseling. Ultimately, he was forced to choose to leave of his own accord.

Although Bob hadn't tried to convert his family, his father observed changes in Bob's behavior that prompted him to call the Cult Awareness Network, a national cult-monitoring organization. It reported that the Boston Church of Christ was on its list of dangerous groups. Six months earlier, father and son had planned a Thanksgiving trip to Chicago, but now Bob's father made some extra arrangements. When the two arrived in Chicago, exit counselors were waiting.

Despite the intense counseling sessions aimed at helping Bob regain his psychological and spiritual balance, when he returned home he tried once more to connect with the group. "After the intervention, I believed the group had just been mistaken about some things," he says. Bob was certain that once he pointed out the group's flaws to its leaders, the problems could be resolved and he would return. "After talking again to my discipler and the leader of the campus ministry, I almost went back."

"I went to dinner and a movie with these guys," he continues, "and I took my list of problems with me. Throughout the evening they said they wanted to solve my problems. I thought they meant the stuff on my list. Over the course of the night, I learned that it was *my* problems they were talking about solving, not the church's!"

Even though he was involved with the Boston Church of Christ relatively briefly, he feels changed by it. "I probably bounce back more easily than a lot of people, but I hit bottom hard. The hardest part for me was realizing that the people I thought were my friends were just using me as their ticket to heaven."

Al: Living with Regret

Al's catalyst for leaving The Way was his feeling that the group had betrayed him. It still plagued him two years after his departure . During that time, he began to deal with the guilt of putting his children through life in what he now believes is a cult. To keep his family together, he remained in the group, despite his loss of faith.

At the start of psychotherapy, he wavers between anger at The Way and anger at himself. Much of what he says is colored with regret for a past he cannot change.

Al first began to doubt his faith after he moved his family to The Way's headquarters in Ohio. Uncomfortable in the midwestern climate, he requested a transfer to one of the groups' campuses in the western United States. He worked for the organization for two years, his family of six crammed into tiny living quarters.

While waiting for permission to move into a larger house, the family spent two weeks visiting relatives rather than attending The Way's annual gathering in Ohio. On the way back to Ohio, they learned that a member of the sect's inner circle would be occupying the home previously promised to them. "It really upset me," Al says, "that because we took a vacation instead of going to Mecca, they wouldn't let us move. So we moved to Idaho before the rest of the group got back from their annual gathering."

Al's attitude worsened. Although trained as an accountant, he was unable to find work in Idaho, and his family life rapidly disintegrated. He applied for leadership positions in The Way, but his applications were rejected. He says. "I believe my family became dysfunctional because I allowed us to be diverted, rather than standing my ground. We may have overcome the crisis of my apostasy and survived as a family. Maybe I could have persuaded my ex-wife to leave. And my kids, well, they knew I was screwing up when I signed us on."

Susan: Divorcing God

Often members of dysfunctional religious groups feel bitter toward God. They wonder how, after giving so much, He could allow them to be hurt so deeply. Susan, 49, angrily left the charismatic commune nine years ago. "I felt that God was a farce," she says. "The whole experience was the craziest thing I'd ever gone through."

Susan's crisis developed gradually. For three years before her departure, she and her husband wrestled with spiritual issues. The more pronounced her doubts, the more desperately she tried to make sense of fundamentalist Christianity. The idea of rejecting the dogma she'd lived by for most of her life left her wracked with guilt. Once her family moved away from the community farm, however, her self-blame quickly turned to outrage.

"All these wonderful Christians got very angry with us and shut us out, pretending not to recognize us," she says. "Being shunned hurt me a lot." Her emotional pain increased when she learned that rumors about her were being spread in her small New England town. According to one rumor, Susan had quit the Christian community because she and her husband worshipped psychologist Carl Jung. She explains, "We had the complete works of Carl Jung and we were very interested in Jungian psychology. To them, that was sinful. I had stayed up day and night pacing the floor with these people as they went through crises, had cared for their kids. We didn't enter into this community half-heartedly, but when we walked away, they closed the door on us. For five years, the anger I felt was unreal. I had given my body and soul to Christianity, and I felt that it was all a lie."

John: Switching Addictions

Some members find withdrawal from the group so painful that they turn to alcohol and other drugs to dull the pain. Although John remained clean and sober in the Unification Church, he hadn't dealt with the emotional issues underlying his addictions. When a spiritual crisis precipitated by his homosexuality caused him to leave the group, almost immediately he began using again.

Although he learned of the group's true philosophy two months after joining, it took him much longer to learn that the blessing dispensed by Reverend Moon as a reward for spiritual attainment entailed arranged marriage. "You meet the conditions for the blessing without knowing why you're doing them," explains John. "I fasted for seven days, a wonderful experience, but I wasn't aware it was a prerequisite for being blessed. Things are revealed slowly. If you're going with the flow, then you accept what's being revealed. If everything had been told in the beginning, maybe no one would have stayed."

As the time for matching drew near, John panicked. Although he was willing to remain celibate, his homosexuality made heterosexual marriage impossible. Instead of questioning the wisdom of the church, he was certain he had failed. When prayer didn't turn him into a heterosexual, he prayed more feverishly. At that point, he decided to leave but delayed his decision and continued going through the motions. "It was like the end of a romantic relationship," he says. "You know it's going to end, but you stay involved for a while."

In his final days with the Moonies, his sense of failure was eased somewhat because of counseling he received from a high-level leader in the group, the mother of a co-worker. In addition to counseling, she gave John a plane ticket West to begin a new life. He hoped his disillusionment was limited to the New York branch of the church only, but to his dismay, he realized that he could not be true to himself unless he severed his ties with the organization.

After finding a job in a restaurant and saving some money, John rented a tiny apartment. "I had to put my life back together," he says. "I didn't have anything." Eventually he met a lover and they moved into a house together, but John shared nothing about his previous ties to the Unification Church. Haunted by his past, he tried to blot them out with alcohol and other drugs. "I went back into addiction very quickly," he confides. "Alcohol and other drugs were a substitute for the church, a way of hiding from myself. I'm 35, and I'm just finding out who I really am. Only recently have I opened up about my past to a few people. My own family denies that period ever happened."

Years after detaching from the Unification Church and three years into recovery from substance abuse, John is haunted by negative self-talk. "How could I have been so stupid and so weak? Why do you need a group? Why can't you be an individual? I still believe the Divine Principle and Reverend Moon, but I don't believe in the Unification Church. Was I taken in? I don't know!"

Crystal: Finding God Everywhere

When people leave one dysfunctional religious group, often they become addicted to another one. Luckily, Crystal discovered Twelve Step groups and has begun rebuilding her self-esteem.

Crystal and her fellow missionaries fled Colombia when they were persecuted by drug cartels. Returning to the United States, Crystal contacted her sister, who owned a bookstore specializing in recovery books. The subject fascinated Crystal, and out of curiosity she began attending AA meetings and Twelve Step programs for codependents and adult children of alcoholics. The more she participated, the more she identified with the recovering alcoholics she met. Shortly thereafter she came to the soul-shaking conclusion that her relationship with the church throughout most of her adult life had been an addiction.

"I did a complete about-face." she says. "My addiction didn't serve me any longer, but leaving the church was very traumatic. I came back into the system after eighteen years of voluntary solitary confinement."

This new way of looking at her past has triggered a number of painful conflicts, including the church-induced dread of adhering to devil-inspired doctrine. "They're fearful I'm deceiving myself," she says sadly, "but I've spent many hours on my knees reading my Bible and lifting my heart up to God. I believe God has answered my prayers by bringing me into recovery. If I belong to God, He will take care of the devil. The more open-minded I become, the more I see God everywhere."

She believes that the rigid doctrines of her church limit a healthy notion of God by condemning therapy and AA groups. "My perception is changing," says Crystal. "I feel God is leading me to listen to people's hearts. The people I've met at AA meetings truly have a relationship with God. God has shown me He can't be confined to doctrines. Jesus loved Peter, and Peter swore. Jesus loved Judas even though Judas betrayed Him."

Crystal's new concept of a forgiving God runs counter to the teachings of her former church. In retaliation for her beliefs and her involvement with Twelve Step programs, her fellow missionaries have shunned her. "They don't talk to me, they don't write, and it breaks my heart," she says. "We worked side by side, we worshipped together, we ate our meals together. Day and night we were together. My therapist said they may feel like I'm dead, and they don't know what to say."

Responding to Crystal's longing for fellowship with her former friends, her therapist asked her if she could return to the mission. Although Crystal believes she would be taken back, doing so would mean denying her feelings and recanting her new beliefs. "I feel I'm right on target in my spiritual growth and I can no longer accept their teachings." She pauses for a moment, then adds, "Now I feel closer to the people at the Alcoholics Anonymous meetings than the missionaries I worked with for years!"

Anna: Leaving the Cave

Anna was completely committed to the Holy Order of Mans when it went through an organizational upheaval and closed the center in her city. Because the group had been the focus of her life for so many years, she was grief stricken. Sitting alone in her apartment she cried out, "God help me!" After that anguished outburst, she didn't speak the name of Jesus Christ or talk about God, except in fear, for more than ten years.

Defying the group's ban on psychotherapy, Anna's teacher arranged for her to see a Jungian analyst. That act of heresy eventually led to the teacher's expulsion. When Anna's therapist asked what she wanted from her work with him, she uttered the first word that came to her mind: wholeness. In many respects, she had come full circle, back to the emptiness she had felt before joining the group.

During many months of therapy, Anna learned that spiritual growth differed from psychological work. "Being spiritual had nothing to do with working on the parts of myself I didn't want to deal with," she reflects. "Going into analysis was like starting over." Years later, her analysis complete, Anna has a positive attitude about life. This gives her the chance to live out her spiritual teachings and to work through her psychological pain. "Now I can return a whole person and experience the Christ within," she says. This painful process of growth has taken her fifteen years to accomplish.

Within two years of the community's closing, most of the members had divorced, despite the group's teaching that marriage is sacred. Several of the women became alcoholics. Anna often thinks about those who heeded the group's dictum against therapy. "The spirituality, the energy in a group is like a drug," she warns. "It opens you up, and unless you have someone or some support system to help you process all the changes you go through, you're in trouble. Maybe it's easy to be spiritual because you are in a cave, not the real world. When you leave that cave, you still have to go back into the world and apply what you learned. You must live the spiritual growth you've attained, or you lose it."

Brenda: Facing the Dark Night of the Soul

Brenda felt emotionally paralyzed by her separation from the Sufi-based school she had joined. She knew she had to leave the organization. The longer she stayed, the faster she lost ground emotionally. Confusion, despair, fear, and anger so dominated her waking moments that she feared a complete breakdown. She continued to attend the bimonthly, weekend-long meetings for a year. Although her teacher had instructed students to stay no matter how uncomfortable they felt, he counseled her to leave. Given the horrors of her childhood, she took his counsel as complete rejection. Today she feels it was the best thing he could have done. Had he not suggested she move on, she never would have.

She recalls that pivotal year, when it seemed that all her childhood traumas returned with a vengeance. "I kept going to my teacher's group until I couldn't bear it anymore. All the time he was very concerned, but he didn't know how to help me, and I didn't trust him, so it wasn't possible for him to help."

After she stopped attending meetings, she concluded that spiritual work was stupid and that she would never do it. For a month, she was so depressed she contemplated suicide. "Everything I knew myself to be was defined by that group and I was lost, completely dysfunctional," she confides. "I thought about suicide."

During this dark night of the soul, Brenda felt she was visited by an invisible presence. Years later she still credits it with putting her life together. "Something, maybe an angel, came to me that was gentler than anything I'd ever felt," she says, her eyes filling with tears. "I suddenly loved all my problems. Everything was just as it was before, but I adored all the parts of my life, even the group I'd left."

After this experience, Brenda began to view her work as an activity director for a nursing home differently. Rather than viewing it as simply a way to earn her living, the job became a spiritual practice for her. "No matter what happens, working with the elderly will continue to be my path. It is the part of my life that is most real," she concludes. "The ideas I learned in the group were useful, but it was when I watched a woman die in the home that I truly started believing in God."

Gary: Moving On

Gary had lived in the Divine Light Mission ashram for two years when the group lost its lease and Maharaj Ji ordered members to make different housing arrangements. Once outside the group setting, Gary realized that although the movement was starting to dissolve, he didn't feel any less spiritual.

Shortly afterward, an allergic reaction to an immunization left Gary comatose for more than a month and hospitalized for many more. When he regained consciousness, he was informed that the mission could not take care of him after he was released. As he recuperated, he began to put the previous eight years into perspective. "Here I was, being fed through a tube in my nose, not attending meetings, not sitting in a lotus position for an hour every night, not doing all the things that I had been told were important," he says. "And I was not feeling spiritually the worse for it. As far as I could tell, I was still growing spiritually and personally."

He doesn't claim that his disillusionment was painless. Being stripped of illusions never is. But he is alive, and wiser than before. "Finding out that everything was not as I'd thought didn't leave me bitter or feeling that I was the victim of malicious abuse," Gary says. "It was awful, but I learned from it. The important thing is not to avoid making mistakes, but to be able to say, 'That was a mistake, and I've learned from it.'"

CHAPTER ELEVEN

Healing from Spiritual Abuse

Members who choose to leave dysfunctional religious groups, are asked to leave, or experience an intervention and exit counseling share common feelings as they heal. After an intense emotional commitment to a rigidly authoritarian organization, those who leave often struggle with a sense of emptiness. Depression, loneliness, alienation, confusion, passivity, and self-imposed isolation are also typical aftereffects of religious addiction and religious abuse.

Especially frightening are the memory losses some members experience after breaking from a dysfunctional group that has used high-pressure tactics to mold and manipulate them. They may develop a tendency to automatically stop critical thinking by praying or chanting, or they may suffer spontaneous altered states of consciousness called "floating." Bible verses or sayings they learned in the group may pop unbidden to mind. These symptoms, although they may frighten religious abuse survivors into thinking they are crazy, are very common among survivors. Like spiritual posttraumatic stress syndrome, they are a reaction to the survivor's experiences. Given time, they do go away.

For many months after severing ties with a dysfunctional religious group, survivors may alternate between certainty that they betrayed the group and absolute conviction that their religion betrayed them. One minute they feel sure that leaving the group or the faith was the best thing to do; the next minute, they are frightened that their departure will doom them to an eternity of unenlightenment or even damnation.

Adults involved in groups that required full-time commitment may lack employment, a place to live, and financial resources. It is difficult to make decisions on their own. As a direct consequence of their misplaced trust, their faith in God may be shattered. To compound the problem, many survivors feel stupid or ashamed for having succumbed to spiritual seduction. It is no wonder, then, that the suicide rate among defectors is high. Without counseling or a self-created program of healing, survivors are especially vulnerable to victimization by yet another dysfunctional religious group.

Some survivors deny the depth of their woundedness. It was no big deal, they tell themselves and others. Silently they pick up the pieces of their lives or they sweep them under the rug, and membership in the group becomes a secret. Rather than learning from the past, they continue to operate with the same frantic patterns of stuffing feelings.

Oftentimes we keep the past to ourselves because we are afraid others will judge us harshly. What would our friends think if they knew we testified at revival meetings or that we'd dropped out of college to join the Krishnas? Would they still be our friends? Susan says: "There's a tendency to think of us as inferior, dumb, and weak. Really, we're just human beings who happen to be vulnerable. The fundamentalists and cults are well schooled in getting people who are vulnerable, going through a divorce, or in transition from high school to college. Ministers and priests don't realize that healing from these groups is an issue. They think, if it's church, it can't be that bad."

Acknowledging Pain

Healing from religious abuse takes time, but it is well worth our patience and effort to go through the stages. Most people work through their hurt, fear, anger, and self-blame to come to a place where they can accept the past and live in the present. Moving beyond black-and-white thinking, they can acknowledge the negatives and the positives of their encounters with a spiritually limiting group. Only then can they integrate the experience into their lives.

The first step toward healing religious abuse is acknowledging the severe emotional, physical, social, and spiritual damage we have suffered. It was real and it hurt! Only when we admit we have been wounded can we admit that we need to heal and then allow ourselves the time and loving care it takes to adjust.

For some survivors, involvement with a religiously abusive group parallels substance addiction. Others find that old childhood wounds are reopened. Still others face the emotional problems set aside when they joined a dysfunctional religious group. Researchers compare the traumatic aftereffects of dysfunctional religious groups with those felt by victims of long-term domestic violence or child abuse. If we try to put what happened behind us too quickly, before we've had a chance to heal, we risk allowing it to subconsciously dictate our lives for years to come.

Coming to Grips with Grief

No matter how much survivors were damaged in their relationship with a dysfunctional religious group, they may cling to their group identity because they're familiar with it. To let go completely means to face the unknown. No matter how their departure from the group came about, they have lost a major part of their lives and they need to grieve the loss. All at once, they are letting go of a belief system, a social system, and a way of life.

Like a divorce, the bonds are broken on many levels. The emotional hooks are deep. Even though survivors may have physically separated from the group, they usually retain emotional ties for a longer time. Like John, they may remain devoted to a former teacher well after they have ceased to be an official member of the group. Others experience ambivalence, switching from love and longing to fear and loathing each time they remember their spiritual mentor. They may privately continue the prayers and rituals. Feelings of sadness are normal.

As survivors sort through their experiences, they need to keep in mind that healing from religious abuse does not mean totally repudiating the group's teachings or embracing their opposite. In fact, some will continue to believe many of the positive things they learned in the group.

In the long run, many survivors regain their spiritual balance, but not without a struggle. The length of time it takes religious abuse survivors to heal depends on the length and intensity of their involvement with the group. If they experienced the abuse in adulthood and it was relatively short term, they may feel cynical about all things spiritual for a time. If, like Susan, they were raised in a religiously abusive environment, they may cling to their anger for years because it serves as defense against further hurt.

"About four years ago, Fundamentalists Anonymous asked me to start a group here," says Susan. "I was so angry with God, I didn't really care whether others got over it or not, so I didn't start a group. A year later, two calls came within a week from people with experiences similar to mine, and we started meeting. They suggested we run an ad in the local paper and things grew."

For two years Susan focused on her emotional issues in the Fundamentalists Anonymous group, but she still hurt spiritually. Several months ago a young man attended the meetings, and he gave a different perspective on religion. "He was a great guy and had a positive way of talking that made me feel hopeful," she explains. "After our meetings we'd go to Denny's and talk. He was a priest and was interested in Fundamentalists Anonymous because a number of Catholic Hispanics in his parish were being recruited by fundamentalist churches. I gave him a hard time because I was still battling with Jesus," she explains. "He was very patient and said God was loving. I'm sure somewhere in my past I'd heard about God's love, but it was overshadowed with sin and evil."

Before the priest moved away, he suggested Susan see a spiritual director. At first she refused, terrified that once more, she'd be giving up control of her thinking. "It's very important for a people to retain the ability to think for themselves," she says. "I'm not about to give that up again." After a month of internal debate, Susan met with the director, and to her surprise, he didn't care what her religious views were.

"My progress with him has been slow and painful. But I believe it is possible to have a relationship with God," she reports. She made headway until he suggested she read the Bible and pay attention to the feelings it evoked in her. "It was like the rug had been pulled out from under me," she says. "I was reading the Bible through the same glasses I had when I was a child, and I felt condemned and worthless. As much as I don't believe you're supposed to read the Bible that way, it's programmed into my head."

Susan is convinced that dysfunctional religious groups target more intelligent people because they have more to give to the group. Once inside a group, however, curiosity is systematically squelched, and mental abilities are channeled into approved directions. "When I was an art therapist, I battled with the whole thing personally. I was a little schizophrenic because I could compartmentalize my life," she explains. "I could go to work and find psychology interesting, but the Christians I knew always censored psychology. There were certain things they didn't want you to know. Whether a fundamentalist group or a cult, it's the same mind-set and it affects people in the same way. You give up your mind and your soul."

"It's not good enough to go to a self-help group unless you're committed to staying with it because healing takes so long," concludes Susan. "You don't come out of it easily. The wounds are so deep, even exit counselors struggle to get you out. They don't really change your thinking. I think I'll be in this process all my life. It took me forty years to get out, and it will probably take another forty years to sort through it all."

Learning to Trust

Time in growth-stifling groups taught survivors that it isn't safe to speak their true feelings. They're afraid that if they talk to a psychologist or counselor, they'll be judged. Although some mental health workers are judgmental, many are not. We can minimize the risk of being judged by contacting a national self-help group that deals with religious abuse (listed under "Resources" in the back of this book). Before we commit to therapy with a counselor, it makes sense to ask about the person's views on spirituality and mystical experiences. Is this person antireligious? Does she have a religious viewpoint she will impose on us? Asking questions up front provides survivors with the information they need to make the right choices.

People who have been scarred by dysfunctional religious groups are extremely wary of any organized groups. Even the most innocent groups may seem sinister. But because such groups provide critical emotional support and understanding, survivors may need to join one or form one. They give them a safe place to express anger and begin working through their hurts. They also provide survivors with nonjudgmental acceptance from others who have shared experiences similar to theirs.

Crystal, like Susan, has found recovery from religious addiction to be a time-consuming and effort-filled process. "Wounds from being in a dysfunctional religious church are deep because religion deals with our spirits—the depth and core of our being," she says. "It's been like being an alcoholic: You have to hit bottom. When you do, and you begin to reach out to God, He'll show you what to do."

Crystal believes that God led her to a Twelve Step program. Even though such programs don't overtly address religious addiction, they do provide a framework for healing. "I don't know what I would do without the support groups. As I read recovery books, work the program, write, talk, feel, and grieve, I begin to get comfortable with myself and love myself. I know that I have to find self-worth within myself, not outside, in a group, not even in AA. My spirituality is more real to me than it was before, and I'm better able to look at the truth about who I am."

Crystal says a more open-minded approach to spiritual seeking has helped her to forgive herself and to picture God as a more loving entity. "I don't interpret Him as being like my father anymore. I've learned to forgive myself. I deal with my bitterness and resentment through the Twelve Step program. I sometimes just sit silently, and God honors it. Even if I go to a meeting and it is painful, I still grow because of it."

Reaching outside the church for help was probably the scariest step Crystal took. "At first I felt I did many things that were unacceptable to the church," she says. "But God reassured me that I was on the right track. It's very important to communicate with people outside the church. People are warm and beautiful, and the church doesn't have all the answers. God doesn't want us to role play; He wants us to be free, happy, and good. When you've had many wounds inflicted, you need to heal starting on the inside."

Breaking Free from Perfectionism

Healing involves facing and working through the issues that may have driven survivors to join a dysfunctional religious group. Whether they struggled with a career change, divorce, addiction, or an imperfect family, those painful underlying problems remain to be resolved. If they blame all of their discomfort on breaking ties with the group and turn their backs on other issues, healing isn't complete.

It's a good idea to get help from of counseling or a support group. Alcoholics Anonymous provided John with the moral support and encouragement he needed. He was able to honestly acknowledge the family history that set him up for religious addiction and to move from seeing himself as a victim to a living survivor.

"My recovery from using alcohol and other drugs began three years ago this next month," he says. "I hit bottom. It was either die or change. My last drunk wasn't the worst one I ever had, but it was the one that woke me up, the one where God said, 'You're right on the edge. You can either step back or go over; it's your choice.' Fortunately, I've been able to remain substance free since then."

His growth now is steady. "The Unification Church was the first real milestone in my life, and I don't remember much about how I was before then," he says. "There are very few people who have that common bond and I still treasure it in a way. Now I use the Twelve Steps more than I do the Divine Principle. The Twelve Steps are different, very individual. I'm never going to be fully recovered. It's a process."

John believes Twelve Step groups have helped him because they don't expect members to be perfect. "I'm trying to develop my relationship with my Higher Power, who has a sense of humor and is not going to damn me for not being perfect," John says. "I don't do the right thing 100 percent of the time, but I'm not perfect and that's okay. The Twelve Steps and recovery have helped me with that. I don't carry around quite as much baggage."

Integrating the Experience

As survivors move past sadness and anger and, like John, are able to confront the emotional underpinnings, they begin to integrate into their lives what happened in the dysfunctional religious group. Rather than sealing off her experience with Scientology and letting it fester, Tracy has sorted out the beliefs she wants to keep and has drawn on what happened to her as a way to help others.

"I know a lot of people who allowed it to be a terrible thing, and twenty years later they are still bitter. Being a Scientologist wasn't all bad," she says. "For me it was a growth experience. I came out better, smarter, and more capable."

When Tracy and her husband left the group, few others had chosen to do so. Within six months of their departure, however, 176 people left the group. The couple turned their home into a safe house for former Scientologists, feeding them, giving them a place to sleep, and helping them get back on their feet. Tracy credits her "underground escape network" as one factor that helped her heal by causing her to confront issues she might otherwise have avoided.

"I made a lot of friends in Scientology," she says. "I have a bond with those people that can never be broken."

In addition to her new family of choice, Tracy relied on her parents while she reclaimed her life. Had they cut her off during her years in Scientology, she would not have had a place to go when she left the group. "I'm different from other former Scientologists," she says. "I had very loving parents, and part of my inner security comes from that. I know people who are still bitter who didn't grow up in a loving, nurturing environment. Even so, being raised in a healthy family wasn't enough to prevent me from joining Scientology."

For Tracy, taking responsibility for joining the group didn't absolve the Church of Scientology of its abuse. Instead, it freed her to reclaim the power for her own spiritual development and make wiser choices. "If you really know God or are connected to the universe, you can't be bitter," she concludes.

During the years Tracy served as an ad hoc counselor for former Scientologists, she met many people who were crippled with shame about their involvement with a group the media had labeled a cult. "Don't be embarrassed about it," she advises. "Don't feel inferior because it happened to you. The exact opposite is true. You're probably a little more evolved because you dared to go after a goal. You had the bravery to leave society and try something new, and then you had the bravery to get out of a bad situation, so the experience actually says wonderful things about you."

Finding a New Frame of Reference

A key to putting enmeshment with a dysfunctional religious group into perspective is to find meaning for the experience and then to create a way to fit that meaning into our daily lives. For many former group members, this process is more challenging and more rewarding than the time spent within the group. Says Renee, "The Church is apostolic and universal and has all the answers. It has a 2,000-year history, and even a prehistory before that. When I left the convent more than fifteen years ago, I didn't want to talk about it. You don't want to talk in case you're wrong, but over the years as you become more confident it becomes easier."

After Renee left the convent, she worked for a time in the mental health field, where she became unit director of a psychiatric hospital. She immersed herself in this work for four years until she sensed a need to move on. Packing her belongings, she set out for Oregon, where she joined a women's group, made friends, and began to talk about her history as a nun.

"In the women's groups, we told our secrets," she says. "I discovered that when you tell your secrets, you usually find out that others have the same issues. I'd lived with women all my life, but we'd kept our secrets and our shame to ourselves. The secrets kept us separate and alone. When you tell your secrets, you realize what you have in common with humanity."

Her new openness eventually led Renee to explore other varieties of spiritual experience besides Catholicism. She traveled to India, half hoping to find something to take the place of the organized religion she had discarded. She says, "I learned in India that Buddhism, Hinduism, Sikhism, Janisism, and all of the '-isms,' are similar to Catholicism in that they are belief systems. There are people who believe everything they are taught, and there are the mystics who go beyond the surface. Those two levels are in any religion. When I realized that, I knew I could stop looking for something to fill my heart up. All religions have some truth in them, and it's our job to pick and choose and to make up our own spiritual tapestry."

During her years in the convent, Renee's spirituality had been limited to praying and worshipping in church. Now that has changed radically. She explains, "I'm often asked if I miss the ritual. But I'm more spiritual now than when I was a nun. God is a part of me, and I don't have to go to mass to have a sense of the sacred. Integration came for me when I started understanding that life itself is spiritual."

One way she's found to put these insights to use is in teaching an adult education class for recovering Catholics. "A critical part of healing is understanding. The Church is based on politics, leadership, and Western thought," she says. "We're violated by our religious institutions because what they teach doesn't correspond with how they operate. By talking frankly about it, we can heal. I don't think I can take the pain away, but I can say, 'You're not crazy. This is what religious institutions are like and they're not so different from political institutions, the family, or the boss.' This isn't just a Catholic problem. It's one that fundamental and liberal religions share."

Finding the Courage to Continue

Ultimately the spiritual search is an individual and internal one. Sometimes, though, we can find the support we need to continue our growth in healthy religious groups. To condemn all spiritual organizations just because we had a negative experience with one is not a sign of critical thinking, but rather of reactivity.

Gary found a sense of community at a Quaker meeting he attended while still involved with the Divine Light Mission. "It was not a contradiction for me to be involved with both groups," he says. "When the Divine Light Mission ceased to exist, I was then free to be wholly involved with the Quaker meeting." Although he doesn't view his connection to the Eastern group as totally positive, he does regard it as an essential part of his journey. "For my own spiritual growth, I had to believe that someone was God Himself before I'd take it seriously," he explains. "Even though I no longer believe that person is God or is ever going to be, I lived with those assumptions. Now I can accept them or dismiss them experientially, not just academically. Anyone who is willing to accept new things can continue to grow. Sometimes you have to learn the hard way. I entered into a relationship with Maharaj Ji not because I was stupid or malnourished, but of my own free will. It's up to each individual to say, 'That was my decision.'"

Only when survivors confront their experience with a dysfunctional religious group and acknowledge their part in the equation can they take back the power for their spiritual growth. Gary explains,

"Coming to terms with religious abuse is a lot like going through divorce. You have to understand the problem is not love or romance but your own and the other person's limitations. Your choice as an adult is whether you're going to focus on someone else's faults or on what those faults bring out in you. Most of the time, there's not a darned thing you can do about someone else's faults, but you can do something about your own. The first step is to be aware of your faults."

If survivors cling tightly to their anger, shame, pain, and blame for longer than necessary, they risk letting dysfunctional religious groups control their lives long after they've walked out the door. Like adult children of dysfunctional families who refuse to come to terms with what has happened to them and won't move through their grieving, survivors continue to live in the past. When they allow themselves to get stuck in the past and stubbornly let it defeat them or keep them from their own spirituality, they become victims of their own codependency. Before they can take their spiritual journey, they have to let go.

CHAPTER TWELVE

Learning to Discern

There once lived a man who longed to be saintly. Despite the No Pedestrian signs posted, he wandered heedlessly down the shoulder of a busy road. He wore an old, torn robe and went barefoot. His hair was matted, filthy, and full of lice. Beneath his arm he clutched a holy book, and his eyes rolled skyward as he chanted prayers in a language known only to him. A true saint driving down the interstate spotted the poor wretch and pulled his Toyota over to the side to offer the man a lift. But the man who would be holy refused and held out his book. "It says in here, it is always better to walk," he said.

"Those words apply to a different time and culture, when there were no freeways," the true saint replied.

"They were written hundreds of years ago, but I just found this book two months ago," the wanderer retorted. Clutching the book more tightly, he continued on his journey.

Like the wanderer, we are sometimes tempted to embrace religious practices simply because they are different from those we have known. In the pursuit of bliss, we attempt to instantly change our lifestyles to fit a new religious system. We lose ourselves by failing to explore ways to incorporate this new belief system into who we are instead of trying to mold ourselves into the image of the group.

The spiritual search triggers many of the same feelings as intense love relationships. Just as desperately lonely singles tend to look for love in all the wrong places, desperate spiritual seekers often become affiliated with religious groups. When we give up our power and allow others to make or break us spiritually, we may settle for organized groups that do little to meet our needs. Even when we find ourselves enmeshed with religious groups that hurt us, we may be reluctant to leave.

We must undertake our spiritual search with wisdom and common sense. Before we are able to discern which situations, individuals, and groups have the potential to help or harm us, we must love ourselves. God has given us the tools we need—our minds and hearts—to draw us toward growth-promoting spiritual communities and to help us stay in balance on the journey.

Experimentation helps us find our balance. We may go too far in one direction and then in the other. For most people experimentation takes the shape of a spiritual journey. By consciously practicing discernment, we can catch ourselves before we go too far in any one direction.

Codependency Cautions

We need to clearly understand our internal needs. If we're not sure of who we are or how we came to be the way we are, we may eagerly accept without question the answers others provide. Until we've begun to do our psychological or emotional groundwork, our involvement with religion may become an escape. We don't have to be 100 percent emotionally healthy before we begin a spiritual quest, but we do need to be sure our basic physical and emotional needs have been met before going off to the ashram or the retreat center.

Otherwise, we risk involvement in a religious group to gain acceptance, a sense of security, or self-esteem. When we look outside ourselves to find ourselves, we are naturally attracted to the promises of dysfunctional religious groups. The more dysfunctional the group, the more promises it makes and the more it appeals to us as a way to numb psychic pain or fill spiritual emptiness. For codependents, religion in any form has great potential to become an addicting opiate. Once hooked, we mistake misplaced loyalty for dedication, compulsive spiritual shopping for open-mindedness, and recklessness for healthy risk-taking.

No matter what issues we deal with, it is critical to practice recovery and resolve those issues. When we opt for the delusion of instant bliss, we become extremely vulnerable to victimization by spiritual assault.

The Social Factor

We need to become aware of our social conditioning and how it influences our present lives. At school and at home we are told to be team players and to obey authority. Bigotry may teach us we are superior to people who are different from us, and we shouldn't trust them or socialize with them. From national elitism, we learn that people who live in other countries are our enemies. Unless we confront the rigid hierarchies in our society and our world as a whole, we are prone to accept the same dynamics in a spiritual organization. We may tolerate isolation, enemy making, and total submission to authority in a religious group without question. Accustomed to the false sense of security they provide us, we also fail to see alternatives to conformity and blind obedience.

The Value of Knowing Our Values

Before we deliberately seek out a spiritual group or teacher, it helps to clarify our own values. When we haven't thought about which actions foster self-worth and which tear it down, we lack a stable basis for spiritual growth. We need to ask ourselves what we value most, what actions we would and wouldn't take and under what circumstances. Without a sense of personal ethics, we are apt to accept any set of rules a group gives us. If we're told to deceive people to get money, we may do so and then feel terribly uneasy—without ever knowing why.

Discovering Our Beliefs

We can learn about and work on our relationship with the Divine, by reading, talking, praying, meditating, and worshipping in a variety of ways. We can provide ourselves a rich context for spiritual growth. If people discuss the apocalypse or avatars, we cease to be impressed simply because we don't understand their words and stop assuming they know more than we do.

Once we understand the connection between ourselves and our Higher Power, we realize that religious groups, preachers, and teachers aren't necessary for us to be at one with God. We are able to exercise the power of choice. We can say no if it's appropriate.

The Pitfalls of Perfectionism

Finally, we can prepare for our spiritual odyssey by letting go of our need for perfection. Brenda advises, "Everybody's a little neurotic, so looking for the completely non-neurotic group is probably a sign that you're not ready to look. If you think you belong to the perfect group, you're definitely in a neurotic group or else you are very neurotic, yourself. Everybody's paint is peeling a little." Often a search for the ideal religion indicates that beneath the surface lurks an enormous sense of inadequacy. When we find the perfect group, many of its ideal qualities are probably nothing more than products of our wishful thinking. We see what we want to see and believe what we need to believe.

Using Our Heads

When we encounter a group that seems to offer an opportunity for spiritual growth, we can use common sense to assess it. Being totally intellectual can stunt our spiritual growth, but not thinking can have disastrous effects, as well. Upon initial contact with a group, a both-feet-on-the-ground analysis of its teachings and dynamics is the best method for providing clues about whether the group promotes growth or damage. Healthy skepticism doesn't mean coming across like the Grand Inquisitor or a crusading atheist. It does mean attending to and acknowledging our perceptions. It involves self-empowerment and responsibility for our experiences. And when we notice the danger signs of dysfunction, we can leave before we become so enmeshed that escape causes great difficulty and pain.

Danger Signs of Dysfunctional Religious Groups

◆ The group doesn't practice what it preaches. A big gap exists between its ideals and actions.

◆ The teachings are dogmatic and rigid.

◆ The teachings given to beginners are couched in vague generalities, platitudes, and buzzwords. The information is so amorphous that it can't be questioned. (If it sounds too good to be true, then it probably is.)

◆ The group seems preoccupied with recruitment and fund-raising.

◆ When doing what the leader claims is God's will, the group believes the end justifies the means.

◆ Group members talk about their leader as if he or she is God.

◆ The group views all aspects of former life as sinful or irrelevant. This includes talents as well as problems such as incest, abuse, and addiction.

◆ The group claims to hold exclusive rights to the truth. Outsiders are considered spiritually ignorant or evil.

◆ Group members are expected to give up family and friends.

◆ Members are manipulated by being either shamed or rewarded.

◆ The group controls information and social contacts.

◆ The group is rigidly hierarchical.

◆ Women are not treated as equals with men.

◆ Sexual coercion is practiced.

◆ Critical thinking and questioning are forbidden.

◆ The group makes great demands of its members and uses guilt to punish those who do not comply.

◆ The group provides a sense of instant intimacy.

- ◆ Questions are ignored or given simplistic answers based on circular logic.

- ◆ Members are promised a "quick fix" or a miraculous cure.

- ◆ Members are required to make long-term commitments and prove their allegiance by quitting jobs, renouncing family, or giving money to the group.

- ◆ Members use pressure, charm, and manipulation to persuade others to join.

Spiritual Survival Strategies

Reflecting on his involvement with the Boston Church of Christ, Bob advises, "Ask questions from the beginning. Find out who's holding the meeting and what groups they are affiliated with. Is the leader of the group a convicted felon? Ask all kinds of questions, as many as you can think of. If you hear a falsehood, leave and don't look back. Once you get involved and those people become your friends, you ignore the lies." Tracy suggests severing all ties with the group at the first sign of trouble. "If you hear that the group's way is the only way, get out," she warns. "You have to have teachers, but teachers are different from gurus and gods. Teachers impart their wisdom and then they move out of your life. They encourage you to think for yourself and to make your own decisions. If the group leads you to perceive spiritual unfoldment as coming from someone else and doesn't encourage you to make your own spiritual discoveries, then you're on the wrong path."

"Buying into the notion that someone else knows you better than you do is also a danger," adds Anna. "Keep all the things that have been genuinely positive in your life. Don't be quick to throw things away. If it's correct and it's right for you, it'll be balanced. But if somebody says, 'Give away your house, kids, and money because that's part of the process,' don't listen. Keep time-tested friends. Even if they get mad at you and you get mad at them because they don't understand, keep your friends to do reality checks. Also remember that a holy person doesn't want to take you to bed."

Brenda adds, "Any group that tells you that you can't leave or else something will happen to you is abusive. If you're told you're going to be damned or die, the only reason you'll stay in the group after that is that you're afraid of dying or going to hell. Fear is not a good reason to believe in God.

"You're in trouble when you forget about God," Brenda concludes. "God is not defined by anyone else. All I worried about was whether the guru liked this or that, and that anxiety made me forget about God. To receive God, we have to hold ourselves open, and we're not doing that when we put ourselves into destructive environments."

Groups that foster spiritual growth tend to

◆ Encourage self-confidence.

◆ Encourage people to think, ask questions, doubt, and disagree.

◆ Encourage members to take charge of their spiritual growth while providing them with support and guidance.

◆ Encourage tolerance and openness to other religious beliefs.

◆ Respect members' rights to own their histories and emotions.

◆ Allow members to interpret any mystical experiences they may have without imposing the group's meaning on the experience.

◆ Allow members to choose their level and type of involvement.

◆ Coerce, shame, and manipulate.

Using Our Hearts

Ultimately, once we are involved with a group, we must trust the messages our hearts provide. We need to attend to our feelings when we interact with the group's members or leadership.

When we undergo any kind of growth, we are bound to hit rough spots. Occasionally we may feel frustrated, angry, sad, fearful, or discontent. Sometimes spiritual growth resembles therapy in that things have to get worse before they can get better. Long ago, St. John of the Cross called this time the dark night of the soul. Disneyland spirituality may be amusing, but real progress is hard work.

When we're enmeshed in a dysfunctional group, negative feelings build over time, despite our initial positive feelings. Whether the group is damaging or our emotional baggage is pushing us toward religious addiction, only when we listen to and honor our emotions can we take the steps necessary to care for ourselves.

Often, if we share our emotions within a dysfunctional religious group, we are shamed for having certain feelings and are ordered to suppress them. We are told that our doubts prove we haven't tried hard enough. Such a response tells us we're in the wrong place. When we are shamed simply for being human beings, we need to look at the group rather than blame ourselves for having emotions.

Dysfunctional Group Members Feel	Healthy Group Members Feel
Constricted	Expansive
Cut off from God	Connected to God
Fragmented	Integrated
Unclear	Focused
Anxious	Calm
Weak	Strong
Disappointed	Fulfilled
Judged	Loved
Afraid	Trusting
Intolerant	Tolerant
Dishonest	Honest
Hurting	Healing
Rejected	Accepted
Sad	Joyful
Hopeless	Hopeful
Disconnected	Detached but welcomed
Confused	Clear
Overburdened	Light
Shut Down	Open
Resentful	Generous
Stuck	Growing
Enslaved	Liberated
Diminished	Enhanced
Undermined	Supported
Needy and Dependent	Empowered
Manipulated	Respected
Downcast	Uplifted
Starved	Nourished

Uneasy feelings are a sign of disease or discomfort. Maybe it's our own spiritual disease we're upset about, but closer inspection may show we've encountered a diseased group.

Moving Onward, Moving Inward

It's important to be gentle with ourselves and with organized religion. Whether we choose not to join a particular group or we leave one we had previously joined, we were not stupid to take a risk that didn't turn out well. On the contrary, we can congratulate ourselves for the wisdom to leave. At least we took the risk and, more than likely, grew from it. Not all religious groups are harmful. Dysfunctional religious groups do meet some people's needs or else no one would join them.

While Gary lay in the hospital recovering from a car accident, he had a great deal of time to reflect on his involvement with the Divine Light Mission. At first he focused on the group's flaws, but over time, he came to a different perspective. "As clearly as you can see the speck in somebody else's eye, it's the mote in your own eye that you're responsible for," he says. "If you get fixated on groups' shortcomings, you waste a lot of energy blaming other people for what is a universal tendency. For me it was wanting the Santa God to take care of me. Gary believes some of his fellow members shared different motives such as greed or a desire for power.

"I don't necessarily think that wanting those things is evil," he reflects. "Sometimes those things are there simply so the species can survive. It's neither good nor evil; it's simply part of being alive."

People who hope to hook members into their dysfunctional religious groups should not deter us from our spiritual seeking. He concludes, "People don't just get to where they're going and stop; they keep going.

"God is not Santa Claus. And when you realize your leader was lying, you can choose to stay there and spend your energy hating that person, or let go and seek further. Spiritual need can help us let go. Don't blame spiritual need for getting you into the group. Just be glad it wasn't beaten out of you. If you're still breathing, you've got what it takes."

In the end, patience and persistence in the spiritual quest will protect us from danger and from losing faith in God. We can cultivate those qualities by reminding ourselves that no matter how much we long for someone to hand us truth or give our lives meaning, truth and meaning ultimately reside in each of us.

The ancient Chinese told the story of a potter who spent his life searching for the perfect shade of red. He filled all his days learning new technologies and experimenting with new techniques to perfect the crimson glaze his heart desired. Nothing worked. He traveled throughout the country and consulted with other potters. None of them could help him. Finally he came home, sat by his kiln, and was so frustrated he threw himself in. His assistant couldn't find him, although he called and called to him. Eventually, when the kiln cooled down, the assistant pulled out the pots that had been fired. They were the perfect shade of red. The potter, himself, was the very thing he had been searching for.

Afterword

A full moon washes the dry grass and underbrush with silver as we pick our way into the shallow ravine where a fire burns in the earth pit outside the sweat lodge. The November air smells of pine trees and wood smoke. Except for our footsteps and the crackling of the logs, no sound mars the stillness.

This is to be a recovery sweat, a modern twist on an ancient purification and healing ceremony. It is my first encounter with Native American tradition. I am curious and a bit nervous, and when a coyote howls, I jump. Even so, there is a feeling of rightness about being here tonight in the foothills above town. My companion and I hunker down, centering ourselves for whatever will happen.

Firelight flickers across the chalky surface of the buffalo skull on the earthen altar, off the abalone shell, and makes the deeply etched face of the leader of this sweat seem to radiate with otherworldly light. Dressed in Wrangler jeans and high-top tennis shoes, he stretches his feet toward the fire and begins to explain what we're about to do. We wait for others to join us and for the twenty-eight rocks beneath the fire to heat to a glowing red.

"This sacred ceremony is hundreds of years old," he says, his voice low, his syllables measured. "The sweat lodge represents the womb of Mother Earth. We will crawl inside and offer four rounds of prayers to the Great Spirit. It will get hot in there," he warns. "So we'll suffer a little, just a little, and we'll pray. Finally coming out symbolizes being born. Some people feel reborn, but I'm not making any promises." He laughs, gets up, and goes behind the lodge to putter with the water bucket.

I study the faces of my companions. My connection to this event is my ex-husband's former drinking buddy, turned chemical dependency counselor. The friend I've come with is a former writing student from my adult education class who only last year was hooked into a cycle of attending AA meetings every Thursday, then drinking himself insensible every Friday. His progress in recovery has astounded me.

"Hey, anybody bring a drum?" the leader calls out from the darkness. "I walked right out and left mine at home!" He steps back into the circle of light, banging on the bottom of a galvanized pail with the flat of his hand, then retreats, shaking his head. When he returns, he's beating on a five-gallon blue plastic soap bucket with a stick. He nods and smiles. "Sounds pretty good, huh? This will have to do." The blue bucket matches the plastic tarps that have been lashed over blankets onto the wooden frame of the sweat lodge. Looking from "drum" to sweat lodge and back again, I feel my doubts grow.

Three women arrive whose faces have the tentative look of the newly sober, like dreamers trying to sift through reality and leave the world of nightmare. By now the rocks are hot.

One by one, we enter the small opening of the lodge on hands and knees. The last rock is brought into the lodge, and the flap is lowered. Suddenly this space is inky black, the deepest darkness I ever remember experiencing. Eyes wide open, I lean forward involuntarily, straining toward the warmth of the rocks which have yet to warm the frigid air. The prayers begin.

At first our voices are soft and self-conscious, but as the heat builds as more rocks are placed in the pit, so do our sincerity and intensity. Asking for the courage to carry out my visions, my doubts and defenses dissolve, and I feel connected to the ritual and to the others there.

Emerging later, drenched but filled with energy, I bring with me a new realization that life begins at birth and consists of a series of rebirths. Some occur in religious rituals, others in the solitary course of transcending pain. These spiritual renewals come to us in quiet moments as we meditate or watch a hawk slice across the sky, when we do acts of kindness without expectation of gain. Rebirth arrives every morning when we awaken to begin a new day. With every breath, we are created once again. Religious groups and spiritual teachers serve as midwives, extremely handy to have around, but only nonessential assistants. If we remember this as we undertake our spiritual journey, we will save ourselves a lot of trouble.

Bibliography

Andres, Rachel, and James R. Lane. *Cults and Consequences: The Definitive Handbook.* Los Angeles: Commission on Cults and Missionaries, Community Relations Committee, Jewish Federation Council of Greater Los Angeles, 1988.

Anthony, Dick, et al., Ed. *Spiritual Choices: The Problem of Recognizing Authentic Paths to Inner Transformation.* New York: Paragon House, 1987.

Appel, Willa. *Cults in America: Programmed for Paradise.* New York: Holt, 1983.

Benson, Herbert. *Your Maximum Mind.* New York: Random House, 1987.

Cialdini, Robert B. *Influence: How and Why People Agree to Things.* New York: William Morrow, 1984.

Clark, John G., et al. *Destructive Cult Conversion: Theory, Research and Treatment.* Weston, MA: American Family Foundation, 1981.

Coles, Robert. *The Spiritual Life of Children.* New York: Houghton Mifflin, 1990.

Conway, Flo, and Jim Siegel. *Snapping: America's Epidemic of Sudden Personality Change.* New York: J.B. Lippincott, 1978.

Diekman, Arthur. "The Cult of the Spiritual." Association for
Humanistic Psychology Conference Lecture. Stanford,
August 17, 1989.

Durckheim, Karlfried Graf. *The Search for the Master: The Meaning of
Spiritual Guidance of the Way to the Self.* New York: Dutton,
1986.

Ellwood, Robert S., and Harry B. Partin. *Religious and Spiritual
Groups in Modern America*, 2nd ed. Englewood Cliffs, NJ:
Prentice Hall, 1988.

Evans, Hillary. *Alternate States of Consciousness*. Northhamptonshire,
England: Aquarian Press, 1989.

Galanter, Marc. *Cults: Faith, Healing and Coersion*. New York: Oxford
University Press, 1989.

Halperin, David A., Ed. *Psychodynamic Perspectives on Religion, Sect
and Cult.* Boston: John Wright, 1983.

Hassan, Steven. *Combatting Cult Mind Control.* Rochester, NY: Park
Street Press, 1988.

Hoffer, Eric. *The True Believer.* New York: Harper & Row, 1951.

Keiser, Thomas W., and Jacqueline L. Keiser. *The Anatomy of Illusion:
Religious Cults and Destructive Persuasion*. Springfield, IL:
Charles C. Thomas, 1987.

Lessing, Doris. *Prisons We Choose to Live Inside*. New York: Harper &
Row, 1987.

Lifton, Robert Jay. *Thought Reform and Psychology of Totalism.* New
York: Norton, 1961.

MacHovec, Frank J. *Cults and Personality*. Springfield, IL: Charles C.
Thomas, 1989.

Meacham, Andres. "Losing Your Soul to a Cult," *Changes*, September–October 1989: 28–75.

Pavlos, Andres. *The Cult Experience*. Greenwood, CT: Greenwood Press, 1982.

Richardson, James T., Ed. *Conversion Careers: In and Out of the New Religions*. London: Sage, 1978.

Robbins, Anthony. *Unlimited Power*. Ballantine Books, 1986.

Rutter, Peter. *Sex in the Forbidden Zone: When Men in Power— Therapists, Doctors, Clergy, teachers and Others—Betray Women's Trust*. Los Angeles: Jeremy Tarcher, 1989.

Sloat, Donald. *The Dangers of Growing Up in a Christian Home*. New York: Thomas Nelson, 1986.

Streiker, Lowell D. *Mind-Bending*. New York: Doubleday, 1984.

Wright, Stuart A. *Leaving Cults: The Dynamics of Defection*. Washington, D.C., Society for the Scientific Study of Religion, 1987.

Resources

American Family Foundation
P.O. Box 336
Weston, MA 02193
(617) 893-0930

Christian Research Institute
Box 500
San Juan Capistrano, CA 92693
(714) 855-9926

Commission on Cults and Missionaries
Community Relations Committee
Jewish Federation Council of Greater Los Angeles
6505 Wilshire Blvd.
Suite 802
Los Angeles, CA 90048
(213) 852-1234 ext. 2813

Cult Awareness Network
2421 West Pratt Blvd.
Suite 1173
Chicago, Illinois 60645
(312) 267-7777

International Cult Education Program
P.O. Box 1232, Gracie Station
New York, NY 10028
(212) 439-1550

Interfaith Coalition of Concern About Cults
111 West 40th Street
New York, NY 10018
(212) 983-4799

FAIR (former Scientologists)
P.O. Box 11136
Burbank, CA 91510

FOCUS-former Cult Members
2567 Columbus Avenue
Oceanside, NY 11572
(516) 764-4584

Fundamentalists Anonymous
Box 20324 Greeley Square Station
New York, NY 10001
(212) 696-0420

PACT (People Against Cultic Therapies)
P.O. Box 4011, Grand Central Station
New York, NY 10160
(212) 316-1560

Personal Freedom Outreach
P.O. Box 26062
St. Louis, MO 63136
(314) 388-2648

Religious Movement Resource Center
629 S. Howes
Fort Collins, CO 80521
(303) 482-8487

Spiritual Counterfeits Project
Box 4308
Berkeley, CA 94704
(415) 540-5767 (MWF 10-4)

Spiritual Emergence Network
250 Oak Grove Avenue
Menlo Park, CA 94025
(415) 327-2776

Task Force on Missionaries and Cults
Jewish Community Relations Council of New York
111 W. 40th Street
New York, NY 10018
(212) 860-8533

Excerpt from
Breaking the Circle of Satanic Ritual Abuse:
Recognizing and Recovering from the
Hidden Trauma
By Daniel Ryder, C.C.D.C., L.S.W.

I had a conversation with a man who unknowingly may have ventured into the early stages of satanism in Sacramento, California.

He'd known a woman at work for a couple of years. The relationship evolved into a romance. After several, what could be described as regular dates, she began to confide in him things that seemed, well, somewhat bizarre, yet also somehow intriguing to him.

She told him, for instance, one night, that she was Jesus reincarnated, then held out her wrists. There were no apparent cuts, yet both wrists were bleeding.

Another night, reportedly through a series of chantings, she somehow teepathically sent an orgasmic type of feeling into him that he reported lasting almost twenty-four hours. Then, as quickly as it had been sent, she supposedly shut it off while in his prsence. As she was doing this, he said, she flashed what appeared to be a cold— very cold—sinister look. This sinister aspect of her personality he'd never seen before.

And while he was concerned, the orgasmic feeling he reportedly had experienced really hooked him, and he continued to see her.

One day he found a book on witchcraft in her apartment, and took it to a friend, who, at one time, had been involved in the practice of white witchcraft. After looking at the book, and hearing some of the stories, his friend advised him he was possibly being lured gradually toward satanism, and that he should be extremely careful.

Shortly after that, he ended the relationship.

"The whole thing got to really scare me after a while," he said. "And what was even odder was, I had known her for almost two years and in no way suspected she was into any of this."

The man is now in Twelve Step recovery for his codependency issues, and is exploring the dynamics around why he was unconsciously drawn toward this type of person in the first place.

On a societal plane, there are different levels of satanism, and different ways people are drawn into it.

As a cult researcher, Jack Roper said he looks at satanism as the "hub" of much of the occult movement. And according to Roper, there are any number of outside spin-off groups that may desensitize and then draw people toward satanism.

Among influences that may begin to pull some young people toward satanism, Roper cites the game "Dungeons and Dragons," imagery. He also said there are any number of other fantasy role-playing games out now that include occult imagery and terminology.

As a follow-up to the interview with Roper, I went to a store in the Los Angeles area that sells these types of games. Other names of games I came across were "The Restless Dead" and "Death on the Rock." The game covers displayed demons, dragons, snakes, and, well, so much horrifying imagery that I actually felt . . . I don't want to say overwhelmed, but definitely uncomfortable, just being in the store with all these images staring down from the shelves.

Roper said many of the games, designed to be highly interesting, actually can become addictive for a significant number of people. At the same time, they also begin to desensitize people.

At a three-day seminar in Indiana on ritual abuse crime, Roper said a police officer from Albany, New York, presented a case study of a nineteen-year-old who was brutally killed by a satanist. The officer displayed some of the murder and torture warpons confiscated from the satanist. They incluyded various types of daggers, guns, and electroshock equipment. All these are things, Roper noted, that magazines that report on the horror film industry don't hesitate to display prominently each month.

The pornography industry also desensitizes people to satanic practices, said Roper. This includes, along a continuum, anything from hard-core "snuff" films (actual torture and murder), to child pornography, to sadomasochistic "porn," to even more soft-core porn that depicts threesome sex scenes. (Sexual orgies are reported to be a part of some satanic cult ceremonies.)

Another influence, especially on youth, according to Roper's research, is heavy metal music. Some bands sing about hate, death, and social destruction. Some bands prominently display images and symbols that are also sometimes used in connection with satanic cults. These may include lightning bolts, demons, swords piercing hearts, skulls, and Nazi swastikas.

And there's another, more hidden, psychological dynamic to heavy metal attraction as well. If a kid has grown up in a dysfunctional family, especially in a highly dysfunctional one, he or she learns to function in—and actually is drawn to—chaos. This chaos may be represented by music that features erratic, raucous sounds and hard-pounding beats. In adulthood, the same person may be attracted to a crisis-oriented job or stormy relationships.

"Heavey metal speaks to the pain I've been through," Roper said a teen he was working with once told him. The youth was trying to get out of a satanic cult he had been drawn into.

Getting pulled into a satanic cult is often a methodical, well-calculated, and very insidious process. That is, unless you've been raised in a transgenerational cult, and already are programmed.

Roper described what he views as a typical process. The first stage, said Roper, may be an invitation to a party where alcohol and "light" drugs are being used. Invitations come from people designated by the cult as recruiters.

The next step often is to introduce sex into the equation. A prospect is then "fixed up" with another cult member in a sexual liaison. Maybe this happens several times. Then, stronger drugs are often brought in, purportedly to enhance the sexual experience.

Then the recruiter will start to turn the prospect on to occult literature detailing spells and other types of incantations, so the prospect, in essence, can develop the power to win over any woman/man. At this time, the prospect also is introduced to other areas of occult study.

In addition, by befriending the prospect, the recruiter will have been able to determine to what degree someone has experienced life trauma, such as being from a dysfuncitonal family, and they will proportionately "love bomb" the prospect, as some other cults do, said Roper. This essentially entails creating a caring facade, spending a lot of "quality time" with the candidate.

Eventually the prospect may be allowed into the "inner circle," where he or she is exposed to satanism and the ceremonies. And with this, there are generally initiation rites—rites of passage, so to speak.

In the cults made up mostly of younger people, prospects have to "prove their worth" through actions like animal sacrifice. Sporadically in teen cults, humans are also killed.

Another initiation rite, said Roper, is grave-robbing. And initiates are often specifically instructed to take the skull, because the skull is the container for the brain, which satanists believe contains spirit powers. Besides, the skull is also a symbol of death, and death is the ultimate victory for satanists because in death they expect to be with their lord, satan, for all of eternity. Again, they look at hell as desirable.

In 1989, in a somewhat rural town about forty miles west of Cleveland, Ohio, three young men—two aged eighteen and one aged twenty—were indicted for breaking into a cemetery. Excerpts from the *Cleveland Plain Dealer* newspaper at the time read:

> Three Norwalk area residents charged with opening two graves, beheading the corpses and stealing the skulls, were part of a cult that had recently gotten instructions on how to sacrifice babies to satan, Norwalk police said yesterday. "We're taking this very seriously," he [Police Chief Gary Dewalt] said. "They admitted sacrificing small animals to satan. They said they smashed their heads and drank the blood. One of them has mutilated himself with a knife. These aren't just kids fooling around."

Other Books on Abuse and Recovery from
CompCare© Publishers

A Day at a Time
This best-selling daily inspirational meditation classic is an invaluable addition to twelve step recovery.

Audio Cassette	$9.95
Paperback	$7.95
Deluxe Gift	$10.95
Classic Hardcover	$8.95

Daddy, Please Say You're Sorry
by Amber
An incest survivor's poignant account of the need to recognize and heal from sexual abuse.

Trade Paperback	$12.95

Do I Have to Give Up Me to Be Loved by You?
by Margaret Paul, Ph.D. and Jordan Paul, Ph.D.
This classic will show you how to have a deeper, more loving relationship while being true to yourself.

Trade Paperback	$12.95

Out of the Shadows, Second Edition
by Patrick Carnes, Ph.D.
This is the book that first identified and explained sexual addiction. It has been an invaluable asset to recovering addicts, their families, and their friends.

Trade Paperback	$11.95

The Twelve Steps for Everyone
by Grateful Members of Twelve Step Fellowships
This guide will enhance your personal growth through any of the twelve step programs.

Trade Paperback	$7.95

Order Form

Order No.	Qty.	Title	Author	Unit Cost	Total
126-9		A Day at a Time—Audio		$9.95	
001-7		—Deluxe Gift		$10.95	
196-X		—Paperback		$7.95	
000-9		—Classic Rust		$8.95	
262-1		Daddy, Please Say You're Sorry	Amber	$12.95	
064-5		Do I Have to Give Up Me to			
		Be Loved by You?	Drs. Paul	$11.95	
269-9		Out of the Shadows	Dr. Patrick Carnes	$11.95	
201-X		The Twelve Steps for Everyone	Dr. Patrick Carnes	$7.95	
				Subtotal	
				Shipping and Handling (see below)	
				Add your state's sales tax	
				TOTAL	

Send check or money order payable to CompCare Publishers. No cash or C.O.D.s please. Quantity discounts available. Prices subject to change without notice.

SHIPPING/HANDLING CHARGES

Order Amount	Shipping Charges
$0.00 - $10.00	$3.50
$10.01 - $25.00	$4.00
$25.01 - $50.00	$5.00
$50.01 - $75.00	$7.00

Send book(s) to:

Name _____

Address _____

City_____State_____Zip_____

❏ Check enclosed for $_____, payable to CompCare Publishers

❏ Charge my credit card   ❏ Visa   ❏ MasterCard   ❏ Discover

Account #_____Exp. Date _____

Signature_____Daytime Phone _____

CompCare® Publishers
3850 Annapolis Lane, Suite 100 • Minneapolis, MN 55447-5443
(612) 559-4800 or toll free (800) 328-3330